PARSON TO PERSON: THREE THINGS GOD WANTS YOU TO KNOW ABOUT LIFE

RUSSELL NOBLE

Parson To Person: Three Things God Wants You To Know About Life

Parson To Person: Three Things God Wants You To Know About Life

Contents

Parson To Person: Three Things God Wants You To Know About Life

About the Author

Russell Noble received a Bachelor's degree in Theology with a Counseling Certificate in pastoral counseling from Liberty Christian College in 1985 and continued studies at Lincoln Christian Seminary and Lincoln Christian University (2001and 2016) for an MA in Intercultural Studies. He has been an Ordained Minister for the Christian Church and Churches of Christ since 1991. He was a Missionary to Indonesia, where he taught in a training school for ministerial students and lectured at a public university in the capital city of Jakarta on the topic of the principles of Christianity. He has preached in several churches throughout Southeast Asia - including the second largest church in Indonesia (having 17,000 members in 1989). He nurtured, organized, and formed five churches.

Upon returning to the United States, he and his wife Stefany (of Chinese-Indonesian decent) ministered at the First Christian Church of Stewardson, IL, for three years. The author has a passion for the lost that keeps him reaching out and striving to be Christ's hands extended. He recalls a college Internship at Chicago's Pacific Garden Mission (famous for their dramatic radio broadcast called "Unshackled") in this way: I spent many sub-zero nights wandering the dark streets of Chicago under the by-passes and bridges calling out the names of those I knew would never come inside for shelter; still, I called aloud as Jesus searching for one lost sheep.

Russell Noble has been commissioned a Kentucky Colonel twice by two different Kentucky Governors. An honor also held by world-acclaimed Colonel Harland D. Sanders. In 2010, the Honorable Governor Steven Beshear made the commission on his family's efforts to establish the

Commonwealth of Kentucky. Then again, in 2016, the Honorable Governor Matthew G. Bevin extended the re-commission based on religious and political affiliations in promoting the betterment of Kentucky lifestyles. The author notes nothing compares to the promise of a robe and crown, when reaching our final destination. I have, in like manner, learned to respect multi-cultures and peoples of all nations as an accurate Biblical representation of heaven.

Honorable Mention

The Very Rev. Dr John Chalmers

The Very Rev. Dr. John Chalmers: Born: 1952 - Clergyman. Born in Bothwell (South Lanarkshire), he was raised in Troon (South Ayrshire). He began studying chemical engineering at the University of Strathclyde but soon transferred to the University of Glasgow to read divinity. He was ordained in 1979 and served first as Minister of the Parish Church at Renton (West Dunbartonshire) and then Palmerston Place

Church in Edinburgh (1986-95) becoming an administrator for the Church of Scotland, based in their offices at 121 George Street. He was appointed a Chaplain to the Queen in Scotland in 2013, served as Moderator of the General Assembly of the Church of Scotland (2014-15) and Convener of the World Mission Council. He met Pope Francis in Rome in 2015 and, with Francis and other church leaders, he played a key role in seeking peace in Sudan. He also served as Convenor of the Board of the National School for the Deaf, having been involved for more than 20 years. Chalmers was awarded an honorary doctorate by the University of Aberdeen in 2016. His youngest son John-James (J.J.) Chalmers (b.1986) was severely injured by a bomb in Afghanistan in 2011 but won several medals in the Invictus Games three years later. (https://www.scottish-places.info/people/famousfirst4395.html; https://en.wikipedia.or g/wiki/John_Chalmers_(moderator)#:~:text=John%20Chalmers %2C%20QHC%20is%20a,of%20the%20Church%20of%20Scot land).

Thomas Satterwhite Noble

Thomas Satterwhite Noble: (Many of the photos included in the book are paintings by this family artist)

An American painter as well as the first head of the McMicken School of Design in Cincinnati, Ohio.

Born: May 29, 1835, Lexington, KY

Died: April 27, 1907, New York, NY

Noble was born in Lexington, Kentucky, and raised on a plantation where hemp and cotton were grown. He showed an interest and propensity for art at an early age. He first studied painting with Samuel Woodson Price in Louisville, Kentucky, in 1852 and then continued his studies with Price, Oliver Frazier and George P.A. Healey at Transylvania University in Lexington. In 1853 he moved to New York City before moving to Paris to study with Thomas Couture from 1856 to 1859.

Noble then returned to the United States in 1859 intending on beginning his art career. However, with the beginning of the Civil War, as a Southerner, he served in the Confederate army from 1862 to 1865. After the war, Noble was paroled to St. Louis and began painting. With the success of his first painting, *Last Sale of the Slaves*, he received sponsorship from wealthy Northern benefactors for a studio in New York City. Noble lived in New York city from 1866 to 1869, during which time he painted some of his most well-known oil paintings. In 1869, he was invited to become the first head of the McMicken School of Design in Cincinnati, Ohio, a post he would hold until 1904. In 1887, the McMicken School of Design became the present-day Art Academy of Cincinnati. During his tenure at the McMicken School of Design, Noble moved briefly to Munich, Germany, where he studied from 1881 to 1883. He retired in 1904 and died in New York City on April 27, 1907. He is buried in Spring Grove Cemetery in Cincinnati. '(https://en.wikipedia.org/wiki/Thomas_Satterwhite_Noble)

Dedication

This book is dedicated to my loving sister Dorothy Hartley, who always managed to remind me of the fingerprints of God in my life. I am eternally grateful, and she will always hold a special place in my heart.

Also, to a friend and laborer in the Christian faith, Pastor Daniel Kusnadi, whose invitation to follow God's leading, took me to the mission fields of Indonesia.

Finally, to the following:

Ken and Millie Simons, an adorable couple that spent their lives mentoring misguided children.

Mr. Max Edelman (who passed away after 91 years on November 05, 2013) shared his testimony as a survivor of the Holocaust. (All five have passed from this life but will live on in the hearts of many for years to come.

Acknowledgments

Special thanks to the family of Max Edelman and the Jewish communities of Cleveland, Akron, and Kent, Ohio.

Thanks for the step-by-step instructions from my mentor and distance cousin, Dr. Gary L. McIntosh, Ph.D., D. Min. Professor of Christian Ministry and Leadership,

Biola University- http://www.churchgrowthnetwork.com/

I am grateful for the continual assistance of my eldest daughter, Mrs. Sabrina Mears, and husband, Cody Mears.

My wife, Stefany Lili Noble, is equally important for a lifetime of support and our youngest child Regina "Dani" Noble.

Also, eternally grateful for the opportunity to expand the kingdom of God with Campus Pastors of Christ Community Chapel - Highland Square, Akron, OH – Rev. Marshall Brandon and Dr. Matt Koons.

Knowing the words of Jesus in Matthew 19:30 that the 'last should be first,' I am eternally grateful to the Pastor of the House of Prayer, Corning, AR – Rev. Jimmy C. McMasters and his family.

Foreword

Resilience is "the ability to become strong, healthy, or successful again after something bad happens," or "the ability of something to return to its original shape after it has been pulled, stretched, pressed, bent, etc." (Merriam-Webster, 2014).

Nothing inspires the human heart like the real-life accounts of real people undergoing traumatic, near-death, debilitative, or life-altering circumstances and, while enduring pain, humiliation, anguish, or moments of resignation, find within themselves the tenacity to come out from experience better, stronger, wiser, and enriched in ways that would not have been imagined possible. The power of biography is the miracle of human connection through narrative, and the story captivates the imagination and affords us vicarious illumination upon the essential virtues of human drama. Through the power of narrative and biography, Rev. Colonel Russell Noble has offered the world a precious gift.

Rev. Noble underscores for us, through the story of the riveting experiences of Max Edelman, the ubiquitous, pervasive potential of human resilience. Human resilience is a gift of God by virtue of creation, ignited by faith, and sustained by precious others who God places in our paths at the most critical moments. The power of resilience exudes throughout the various challenges of Max Edelman's trials.

Astounding beyond the ordinary is how human resiliency, when utilized in tandem with the mysterious, providential care of God, enables one to survive cataclysmic tragedy, even when most, if not all, of the protective factors that ensure resilience to existing are gone.

The story to which you are about to be exposed bears significant similarity to the experience of One who, against all odds, amid the most heinous brutality known to humankind, endured suffering to the end and came out victorious with resurrection triumph.

On the other side of "through," we may come out scarred, battered, or diminished in various ways, but we do come out! We emerge from the fruit of resiliency changed forever, either bitter or better. I pray that your engagement with Rev. Russell Noble's workplace you in the course of ensuring that your life is littered with the essential elements that make resilience possible. Your destiny is at stake! Read this book through to the end and be reminded of the spiritual affirmation of the Apostle Paul, "I can do all things through Christ who strengthens me." (Phil. 4:13, KJV)

Forward by Dr. Kilen K. Gray, Dean of Students at Louisville Presbyterian Theological Seminary, Pastor of New Mt. Zion Baptist Church, Shelbyville, Kentucky (25 plus years). Dr. Gray and his wife Cassandra Gray are co-founders of Creative Spirits Ministries, a counseling community ministry. Dr. Gray, a native of Memphis,

Tennessee, graduated with honors from George Washington Carver High School and a graduate of Kentucky State University (Bachelors of Science degree in Computer Science).

He received a Masters of Divinity from the Louisville Presbyterian Theological Seminary, Louisville, Kentucky, and D. Min. (May 2015). Photo: Reverend Kilen K. Gray and Reverend Cassandra Harris-Gray

Introduction

The purpose of writing this book is to inspire Christians to reflect Christ by living lives with true resiliency in their identity, purposefully happy, and most of all, to have a focal point for their destiny. These three elements have been infused within all of us by our Creator God and exemplify His loving kindness towards us. The book's central theme has three things every Pastor should convey to their congregation about what God intends for their lives.

Three things that God wants you to know about life: To be strong and courageous (resilient); to genuinely be happy, you must cultivate an attitude of gratitude, and in looking into the future, it is Gods will that you become conformed into the image of Jesus Christ (destiny). I believe we are in a period of fermentation within the church that is unmatched by any other time in history (aside from the first century).

God wants the church to continue to point people to Jesus Christ, and even though we are persecuted, we should have the inner peace which allows "the joy of Lord" to become our strength (Psalm. 28:7).

Let it never be said that Christianity no longer resembles the personality of Jesus Christ.

Most historians believed that Jesus Christ lived on the earth for approximately 33 years and was crucified by the Romans under Pontius Pilate.

During the first century, Jesus Christ had a group of followers who among the closest were twelve men he commissioned to spread the gospel- "good news" to all the nations (Matthew 28:18-20).

By closely examining the lives of these men, we can find that none of them were scholars or rabbis. None of these men had any extraordinary skills or abilities. Aside from Luke, a medical doctor, and Paul, who studied under the famous Rabbi Gamaliel, none of these men couldn't even be considered academic, let alone religious. The men and women of the Bible were far from socially refined; they were just ordinary people given an extraordinary task.

In John 16:7-9, Jesus tells them how they will be enabled for such an extraordinary task. "But I tell you the truth; it is to your advantage that I go away; for if I do not go away, the Helper will not come to you, but if I go, I will send Him to you. And He, when He comes, will convict the world concerning sin and righteousness and judgment; concern sin because they do not believe in me...."

The Holy Spirit, who had in times past been a force of God's mighty power and excellence, has now come to live in the hearts of every believer (in Acts 2).

Following this event, a radical transformation changes the course of human history and impacts the future to where you and I presently live (and beyond).

The Apostle Paul describes it best in the following verses- please note the use of the word "glory" in both passages.

2 Corinthians 3:17-18 says: "Now the Lord is the Spirit, and where the Spirit of the Lord is, there is liberty. But we all, with unveiled face, beholding as in a mirror the glory of the Lord, are being transformed into the same image from glory to glory, just as from the Lord, the Spirit."

Colossians 1:27 says: "To them, God has chosen to make known among the Gentiles the glorious riches of this mystery, which is Christ in you, the hope of glory."

In both of these passages, the English word "glory" translates into the Greek word Doxa and means the manifested (excellence) of God (Strong's Concordance, 1391, 2004 - 2013 by Biblos.com).

Can you get excited about what that means in the lives of every believer in Jesus Christ? It means that the power of the resident Spirit is transforming Christians into the image of Jesus Christ. It is a transformation that reflects God's manifested (excellence) to a fallen world. That doesn't mean perfection, but it does mean completion!

As we walk upon the earth, we can become "candlesticks of light to this world," allowing all to behold God's love and divine nature, or we can become obstacles and a spiritual force to be reckoned with.

In the course of our journey, we will inevitably collide with the "powers and principalities of darkness within this world" (Eph. 6:12).

As for the adversities, they will seek great havoc and destruction upon our lives. As followers of Christ, we must remember the words of Jesus in John 16:33: "I have told you these things so that in me you may have peace. In this world, you will have trouble. But take heart! I have overcome the world."

Theology shows us that God does nothing prematurely, as he can foresee the beginning from the ending. God waits until everything is ripe for the execution of his purposes.

Galatians 4:3-5 reads: "But when the fullness of the time had come, God sent forth His Son, born of a woman, born under the law, to redeem those who were under the law, that we might receive the adoption as sons." (NKJV)

During an appointed time ascribed upon the eternal calendar of God the Father. Jesus Christ came into the world as a helpless child and, after 33 years, went to a cross and died as a substitution for the world's sins. Then with a blast of physical power (in Greek, it's dunamis- the same English word derived from "dynamite") from God, he rose from death to live forever. (Strong's Concordance, 1411, 2004 - 2013 by Biblos.com)

Romans 8:3 and 4 illustrate to us how God waited for the right time and fully executed His perfect plan.

For what the law was powerless to do because the flesh weakened it, God did by sending his own Son in the likeness of sinful flesh to be a sin offering. And so, he condemned sin in the flesh, so that the righteous requirement of the law might be fully met in us, who do not live according to the flesh but according to the Spirit.

Jesus Christ was born to Jewish parents subject to the Torah (and the Laws). He kept the festivals of Moses, and following his birth, Joseph and Mary circumcised him on the eighth day. Clearly and emphatically, Jesus Christ was "made under the Law." The Hebrew phrase is "yelled isshah," which denotes that a child is "born of a woman." This phrase also implies that a human being was formed in the womb and was meant to illustrate the humanity of Jesus Christ. He was considered a Hebrew under civil and judicial law. This, in turn, teaches us to be in subjection to earthly civil magistrates that rule over us even though they are corrupt in all appearance; Paul tells us they are ordained for God's eternal plan. (Romans 13:1) Many have said that Jesus Christ has put a period to the end of a term and fulfilled its purpose.

The individual gives a genuine testimonial in the story you read and focuses on historical sources. It is meant to show an example of a lifestyle of human resiliency and the strength to overcome within the community despite overwhelming odds. It is up to you, the reader, to visualize the circumstances and, with foresight and imagination, follow the story to its conclusion. You must realize that history cannot be rewritten and that the individual's personal choices are only part of the conclusion. Follow the choices made and how each situation was orchestrated for the person's well-being and God's ultimate glory. King Solomon so graciously conveyed that God's wisdom cannot be reconstructed: "What has been will be again, what has been done will be done again; there is nothing new under the sun." Ecclesiastes 1:9 NIV

A note to the skeptic regarding divine intervention let us give it the benefit of the doubt. That is to say, while you are defining the meaning of truth, please consider biblical truth as an option. Current world trends have selected "relativism" as the most popular definition of truth. This popular definition considers all points of view "equally valid and relational by each perspective." In other words, truth to you may not be the truth to me. The definition of truth by this standard is in and of itself a contradiction. Truth by this equation would dissolve in the process of filtration from person to person.

If God is involved in our lives at all, it is solely based on establishing the truth and transforming us into the likeness of His Son Jesus Christ. Dr. Jim Colledge defines reality in this way: "Truth stands independent of anything or anyone. It is grounded in the nature and character of God, and has been revealed in the Bible."

From a Christian perspective, the Apostle Paul admonishes his audience in the book of Colossians 2:8 NIV – See to it that no one takes you captive through hollow and deceptive philosophy, which depends on human tradition and the elemental spiritual forces of this world rather than on Christ. I would also challenge you to read provocatively, asking yourself engaging questions like: what would I have done, or how would I have responded under such circumstances? You might find a resolution to a problem with a common thread.

Concerning the testimony of Max Edelman as it was given before his death, I testify to the best of my knowledge (reviewed by his family) that it is accurate, and the sources surrounding it have been documented. My wife and I spend several hours (and days) reviewing the writings for his approval. After making slight changes, Max conveyed that he was excited to read the book in its entirety and had no problem with our audience being primarily Christian.

Please remember that I do not intend to change his testimony or even alter it to create a false conclusion. I also caution you as a reader to give Max and his family and the whole Jewish community the respect they deserve in cultural and historical content.

Let us read, intently as situations will quickly unfold uniquely. Many of these situations are from a human perspective, "void of all hope," yet they transform themselves into appealing displays of beauty in a moment. The transformation process by a common Scottish phrase would be noted: "from thorns to thistles."

Chapter One

<u>The Polish Exile</u>

The Max Edelman Story:
Harps by the Willow Brook

Max Edelman is a man who has faced countless losses and pain that many of us can't even begin to imagine. Born in Poland on September 26, 1922, he came from a devout Jewish family.

He was a man of principle and strength, and coming from a family who was very close with their religion had to face unspeakable horror. He was targeted for who he was, being beaten by his peers while also experiencing anti-Semitism from his teacher.

World War II was a time of great conflict and barbarism for people worldwide, especially for the Jewish community, as many of them were murdered, tortured, put into gas chambers, and separated from their families. The fire stoked by Nazis reached the small town where Max Edelman lived. In September 1939, the Nazis entered the village, and the first experience of loss he faced was when they murdered his rabbi.

Sadly, this was only the beginning as Edelman and his

family were moved into a ghetto, soon after being sent to a small concentration camp where he had to work in an airplane factory. Max Edelman's life was one of slavery, where he had to work daily under extreme conditions in the camp. He put his head down and worked tirelessly so that he and his family could survive, yet it wasn't enough.

On April 8, 1944, the Nazi guards beat him like animals, leaving him almost on the brink of death. The agony he faced during this time was unspeakable, yet there was hope deep within him even though, in his own words, this was the most devastating moment in his life.

With the injuries he sustained, his friend, who was a doctor, started treating him, but he had little to no equipment, and sadly because of the damage sustained to his eyes, he slowly started to lose his eyesight.

He was then moved to Flossenbürg to work in another airplane factory, and as time passed, he slowly started to not recognize the objects around him. And one day, he woke up to realize he was completely blind. During his captivity at Flossenbürg, he was protected by his barracks supervisor, who created a hiding place for him. Max was starting to lose hope, but his friend pushed him to keep fighting even when he was sent on a death march in April 1945. He was finally free, but the cost of him losing so much took a toll on him. This was when it happened. On April 23, 1945, the American Army liberated him.

His story can be described as tragic, but no, it was one of resilience as he came to terms with being blind and soon after got married, became a physical therapist at a school for the blind in Germany, and finally immigrated to the United States of America in 1951.

Max Edelman finally passed away at the age of 91 in 2013. His story is one of hope, triumph, and, most importantly, resilience, which is also at the heart of this book

The Trinity of Elements

The divine purpose of writing this book is to inspire Christians worldwide to reflect Christ by living lives with true resiliency in their identity, purposefully happy, and most of all, to have a focal point for their destiny. These three elements have been infused within all of us by our Creator God and exemplify His loving kindness towards us.

The book's central theme has three things every Pastor should convey to their congregation about what God intends for their lives. Three things that God wants you to know about life: To be strong and courageous (resilient); to genuinely be happy, you must cultivate an attitude of gratitude, and in looking into the future, it is God's will that you become conformed into the image of Jesus Christ (destiny).

I believe we are in a period of fermentation within the church that is unmatched by any other time in history (aside from the first century). God wants the church to continue to point people to Jesus Christ, and even though we are persecuted, we should have the inner peace which allows "the joy of Lord" to become our strength (Psalm. 28:7). Let it never be said that Christianity no longer resembles the personality of Jesus Christ. So begins the journey of understanding Christ and our purpose and destiny through it.

How Can We Sing the Songs of the Lord While in a Foreign Land?

There is nothing more exuberant than being surrounded by your people in a place where you know that you will be taken care of no matter what. You will always feel like a foreigner among the populace that does not share your faith and belief. This is how our story begins, with a title taken from the Old

Testament book of Psalm 137:1-9 NIV, where it so beautifully laments the formerly dramatically:

By the rivers of Babylon, we sat and wept when we remembered Zion.

There on the poplars, we hung our harps,

For there, our captors asked us for songs, our tormentors demanded songs of joy; they said, "Sing us one of the songs of Zion!"

How can we sing the songs of the LORD while in a foreign land?

If I forget you, Jerusalem, may my right hand forget its skill?

May my tongue cling to the roof of my mouth if I do not remember you if I do not consider Jerusalem my highest joy.

Remember, LORD, what the Edomites did on the day Jerusalem fell. "Tear it down," they cried, "tear it down to its foundations!"

Daughter Babylon, doomed to destruction, happy is the

> *one who repays you according to what you have done to us. Happy is the one who seizes your infants and dashes them against the rocks.*

This hymn is commonly attributed to the Jewish prophet Jeremiah by Rabbinical sources and used by many Eastern Orthodox Christians. It expresses the yearnings of the Jews during the exile of the Babylonian conquest of Jerusalem on March 587 BCE. The psalm begins with the historical rivers of Babylon, the Tigris River of Mesopotamia, and the Euphrates of eastern Turkey, both flowing through the modern regions of Syria and Iraq.

The ancient city of Babylon was known for its rivers, as they were equivalent to our modern highway system. In Genesis 2:14, the Euphrates was one of the four rivers flowing out of the Garden of Eden, along with the Pishon, Gihon, and Tigris. The river Euphrates also marked one of the boundaries of the land promised by God to Abraham and his descendants. They utilized these waterways for transportation, commerce, and leisure.

When this psalm was written, King Nebuchadnezzar II had just conquered Judah and Jerusalem. History credits him with the construction of the Hanging Gardens of Babylon. Architectural mastery such as this could only translate into the struggle of slave labor for these exiled Jews. These Jews were, without a doubt, forced laborers, resting from a burdensome task.

The text says: they "sat down." They purposefully came together as a group, and now with melancholy hearts, they considered the songs of Zion. The Jewish enslaved people were of a common heritage and interest, as they bewailed and lamented together. This was not just another pity party or tearful display of the silent kind; they were overcome with grief. The text shows the perfect mood and tells us that they wept until they could not weep anymore. They cried themselves out.

The Jewish people are known for joyous celebrations, and the harps were instruments often used in the temple services. Their intent must have been to worship God as they rested along the riverside, but they couldn't hold the tears back when their captors asked them to sing the songs of joy.

In American culture, we often talk about singing the blues when struck with grief, but the text says they couldn't even stand the sound of the music and began to hang up their harps for yet another season. The tears somehow revitalized their patriotism, but that wasn't enough as they had become overwhelmed with sadness.

They must have also felt they were being accused and mocked by their captors because here they sat, tired, tortured, and far away from their people, yet that wasn't enough satisfaction for their captors. They had lost the melody of life and had reached a place of emptiness and poverty of spirit.

I have encountered people at their lowest ebb in life all across America. The nuances of this life beat down many in despair and without hope. Masses are enslaved by addictions or refuse treatment for mental illness. While in Proverbs 13:12, NIV says: "Hope deferred makes the heart sick, but a longing fulfilled is a tree of life." This scripture tells us that many situations of hopelessness and despair begin with disappointment.

The Babylonians had seen the gatherings of these Jews back in Israel and were quite familiar with the instruments of Zion. I can see a crowd gathering to hear what songs they might sing in my mind's eye. The intentions of the Babylonians remain unclear within the text.

It is uncertain whether or not their tormentors were sincere in their desire to hear the songs of Zion or if they were mocking the oppressed. It matters not at this point, as the Jewish people suddenly felt far from home. The psalm reflects the longing for Jerusalem as their native land and the hatred for their enemies with somewhat violent imagery.

From the beginning, their sadness demonstrates the request of their tormentors by saying, "Sing us one of the songs of Zion!" Songs of worship should not be dark and foreboding but happy and rejoicing. Yet these Jews were burdened by the oppression of their captors. They began to ask themselves the rhetorical question, "How can we sing the songs of the Lord while in a foreign land?" Then they commenced by hanging their harps upon the trees along the riverside.

It was at this point I made a remarkable linguistic discovery. As a young student of the Bible, I began memorizing the King James Version with its dated language. It was not until the first pastorate that I discovered the congregation had taken a more modern approach.

So, I began reading Psalm 137 in the New International Version, and upon reading verse two, I found a tree of a different sort. Verse two in the newer translation read, "There on the poplars we hung our harps," while the King James version read, "We hanged our harps upon the willows in the midst thereof." At this point, I'm scratching my head, completely perplexed and asking myself, was it a willow or a poplar?

In several biblical translations, the Euphrates poplar was often mistaken for the willow tree. In appearance, the Euphrates poplar had polymorphic leaves (different shaped leaves on each branch), which appeared as a willow from a distance. In translation, the ancient word Aravah finds a more descriptive meaning in the modern world of Tzaftzafah. Aravah was commonly translated as willow to describe trees of typical design and locations as if I would know that the thirsty willows were often found growing by the riverside. In reality, they weren't willows but poplars, cottonwood, or aspens.

Verse 9, in my opinion, is one of the most graphic and unsettling verses in the entire Bible. It is, however, a prophetic description of Isaiah 13:16 during a time when Babylon murders the descendants of Israel. It says, "Their children shall be dashed to pieces before their eyes; their houses shall be spoiled, and their wives ravished." The

Babylonians horrified the Jews by doing exactly as the text suggested. Then 49 years later, the Medes repeated the same actions in their conquest of the Babylonians.

The grounds of my immense interest in Psalm 137 are not only because I found the text a bit confusing or utterly gripping. But because while I was taking the personal testimony of a dear friend and Holocaust survivor, Max Edelman, I was struck with a sudden and profound feeling of similarity between his emotions and the feelings of Jewish people during the Babylonian captivity.

As the survivors of Shoal (the Holocaust) begin to leave this earth, let us remain faithful to the testimonies we have been given that show God's providence to humanity. As we go forward, I'm confident that you will find many similarities between Psalm 137 and Nazi Germany. Moreover, the psalm points the listener to a covenant-making God and concludes with the promise: "God remembers Jerusalem." The relevance of this psalm and the Max Edelman story is to propagate these characteristics for future generations. If we forget the lessons of our past, they will surprise us in our spiritual slumber and smother us with indifference. Assuredly, they will pump the intensity of hatred and bigotry into our hearts to be repeated.

Bibliography

Others were shot at the Krasnik Jewish Cemetery.

Budzyn Labour Camp www.HolocaustResearchProject.org

Budzyn Labour Camp www.HolocaustResearchProject.org

Worked in Budzyn – as in all the camps I was in – as a joiner. During the construction of the factory, I made, for example, tables and doors, everything expected of a joiner. The head of the joinery workshop was an ethnic German by the name of Karl. He was a civilian. Of the guard detachment, I remember especially well

Budzyn Labour Camp www.HolocaustResearchProject.org

Budzyn Labour Camp www.HolocaustResearchProject.org

And Hantke. There was also one with a name which sounded like Acker or

Budzyn Labour Camp www.HolocaustResearchProject.org

Budzyn Labour Camp www.HolocaustResearchProject.org

When the name Axmann is mentioned to me, then I am sure this is the man I am thinking of. When the name Josef

Leipold is mentioned to me, then I can.

Budzyn Labour Camp www.HolocaustResearchProject.org

Budzyn Labour Camp www.HolocaustResearchProject.org

He was the last Commandant of the camp. He went with us to Brunnlitz.

Budzyn Labour Camp www.HolocaustResearchProject.org

Budzyn Labour Camp www.HolocaustResearchProject.org

I remember that once when we returned from work, the old

Budzyn Labour Camp www.HolocaustResearchProject.org

Budzyn Labour Camp www.HolocaustResearchProject.org

And the children were no longer in the camp. We were told that they were taken out of the camp in a railway wagon – and had been killed.

Budzyn Labour Camp www.HolocaustResearchProject.org

Budzyn Labour Camp www.HolocaustResearchProject.org

On September 15, 1935, the Nuremberg Laws prohibited

THIRD REICH: NATIONAL SOCIALIST RACIAL DOCTRINE - NATIONAL .... Third Reich: National Socialist Racial Doctrine - National Socialism - History - environment - 2022

On August 1, 1936, the Olympic Games opened in Berlin

"The Nazi Olympics Berlin 1936". Ushmm.org. United States Holocaust Memorial Museum. Retrieved 7 October 2016.

"Jewish Athletes – Marty Glickman & Sam Stoller". Ushmm.org. United States Holocaust Memorial Museum. Retrieved 7 October 2016.

Pope Pius XII failed to stand up for the Jews

Ronald J. Rychlak - Wikipedia. Ronald J. Rychlak

During the dedication ceremonies of the Holocaust Museum in Washington, DC, on April 22, 1993, Mr. Wiesel addressed

Elie Wiesel - United States Holocaust Memorial Museum. Elie Wiesel — United States Holocaust Memorial Museum

Chapter Two

<u>The Blind Man in Paris</u>

Pass Me Not, O Gentle Savior

Francis Jane Crosby was indeed a saint as she wrote more than 9,000 hymns, some of which are among the most popular in every Christian denomination. She has written countless hymns and used different names, making sure hers isn't the only name remembered, so pure was her intention and heart. Francis Jane Crosby was a master of her craft, but the most memorable part about her story is that she did all of this even though she was blind.

A preacher once told her that it was a pity that the Lord gave her so many gifts, yet the gift of sight eluded her.

Fanny Crosby responded beautifully by saying that if she could have requested one thing at birth, it was to be blind so that once she passed on and went to heaven, the first thing she would see would be the Lord himself in all his glory.

Born in Putnam County, New York, Fanny Crosby later on would become an American poet. Though her life didn't start off well, to say the least. Fanny Crosby became ill within the first two months of her birth. During this unfortunate event, the family doctor was away, and another man had to be called in. This man, however, pretended to be a certified

44

physician and treated her illness which subsided but left her blind.

He told Fanny Crosby's family to use mustard poultices on her eyes. When it was revealed that the doctor was lying about his qualifications, he ran and disappeared.

A few months later, tragedy struck again as Crosby's father passed away. This event led to her mother having to find work as a maid to support the family. During this time, Fanny Crosby was raised mainly by her Christian grandmother.

Her life is a perfect example of how tragic events can shape your life. Despite all that had happened to her, she still found a way to find the Lord's love. One of her famous hymns was "Safe in the Arms of Jesus." She is someone that many of us should strive to be like.

"Safe in the Arms of Jesus" would be played at the funeral of President Ulysses S. Grant in 1885, and in 1975, long after her death, she would be inducted into the Gospel Music Hall of Fame. Her blindness would never stop her from doing the things she loved most.

Listen to the words of the first stanza and the chorus of the hymn:

"Pass me not, O gentle Savior, Hear my humble cry; While on others Thou art calling, do not pass me by. Savior, Savior, Hear my humble cry; While on others Thou art calling, do not pass me by." Many were the songs and poems of earnest reply, "just to remember me and do not pass me by."

The heart of the hymn is about how Jesus would accept us no matter what. It does not matter where we are and what we have done.

He will embrace us if we call out to him.

None would long for the presence of a liberator quite like those suffering at the hand of their oppressors. While the western world continued to receive reports about inhumane treatment in Europe, propaganda had become a war strategy.

In 1933, Hitler first realized the importance of propaganda and appointed Joseph Goebbels as Minister of Propaganda. Joseph Goebbels was so remarkably effective in obscuring the truth and manipulating the public's mind that Hitler decided to incorporate it into a campaign.

A by-product of propaganda is "brain-washing," which spells multitudes for any dictatorship. After all, propaganda is as old as people, politics, and religion.

Meanwhile, conditions at the Budzyn camp were somewhat bearable (I use the term lightly) due to the efforts of the camp elder and Jewish Prisoner of War, Noah Stockmann. The camp had been initially established for Poles of Jewish origins who were POWs; these had all the best jobs. Elder Stockmann convinced the camp authorities not to retaliate against the Jews on several occasions. In fact, on Passover of 1944, Noah Stockmann managed to get matzo (unleavened bread) baked for a small group during the Seder ceremony.

In May 1944, the Budzyn camp was evacuated, and the prisoners were sent to other nearby camps. Thanks to a Polish Army report from Krasnik dated March 15, 1944, we have the precise number of inmates at the Budzyn camp before this dispersion. The report shows there were 2457 Jews total, including 319 women. Max described the markings each prisoner was forced to wear in the towns and ghettos and the camps that followed. All Jews were forced to wear a yellow Star of David outside their clothing while in the villages and ghettos.

In concentration camps and death camps, the rules were

decided by the commandants of each camp. In Budzyn, we had no markings. The prisoners' numbers were tattooed on the left wrist only in the Auschwitz and Birkenau death camps.

In Flossenbürg, on the other hand, we had the prisoner's number stenciled in black numerals on a white strip of cloth sewn on the left side of the chest and a triangle to the left of the number, yellow for Jews, red for political, pink for homosexuals and black for criminals. My number (recalls Max) in Flossenbürg was 14426. We had tattooed letters KL. In German, "concentration" is spelled with a K, and the word camp in German is Lager, so the letter KL stands for 'Koncentrations Lager.'

In August 1943, the records show that 200 of the camp's prisoners were sent to the death camp of Majdanek. Budzyn was declared a concentration camp on October 22, 1943, and by February 8, 1944, scores of prisoners were massacred by Ukrainian guards. Max and I discussed the daily routine for the camp as I began our conservation with some research, I was able to uncover before our interview. The daily routine at the Budzyn labor camp was as follows:

At 5:00 AM, the prisoners were paraded into the courtyard

and counted. Prisoners were then left to stand for an hour while the SS had their breakfast, and they were given coffee or tea (made from the weeds in the garden or around the camp).

At 6:00 AM, the working parties went to work in the aircraft factory. By noon, it was lunchtime, and the workers were returned to the camp for cabbage soup. All prisoners returned for a meal consisting of cabbage soup and a quarter pound of bread by evening. Following the evening meal, the prisoners went to their bunks, numbered five above one another.

Although they had no blankets, there were so many in each barrack that their body heat was warm enough. The morning beverage for breakfast was optional, either coffee or tea – made from the garden's weeds or surrounding the camp. At this point, Max interrupted me sharply, "It wasn't coffee! It was just brown water, but it was hot, and that's all that mattered."

Then he paused and enjoyed the tea my wife had made before our visit. "I never drank the tea," he added. "The bread… the bread was made from some meal – not Jewish Rye, or wheat – and mixed with sawdust. They never wasted anything."

Then he said, not everyone came to the roll-call. Naively I asked why not, and he blurted out loudly because they were dead! Then he shared, "I recall one instance lying the whole night next to a dead man. I shook him in the morning for the roll-call, calling him by name, saying, 'come on, it's time to get up.' Still, he was lifeless and cold as ice." Max elaborated, "it was some people's job to carry the corpses out of the barracks every morning... and there were always several. They would throw the bodies on a cart and then dump them in a hole."

I asked Max if he remembered any of the commanders of the camps. He said, "Yes, the evilest of all the commandants was in Budzyn, named Reinhold Feiks. He had a whip and wore a revolver. He would bring us in when he entertained guests with a wicked display. Once I was called in and told to make a line of five, I was fourth from the left. Number three was called forward. Feiks had a vicious German shepherd and commanded the dog to attack.

The dog went directly for his throat, crushing the man's larynx and mauling him to death. Then the dog, with blood covering his face, returned to his master for a treat and was applauded for his obedience."

At this point, my wife and I would learn something very personal about our friend Max Edelman. The observe would state that he might develop a fear of dogs after witnessing this German shepherd maul a fellow prisoner before his eyes. The reality was that his fear of dogs would become such an obstacle in his seeing-eye journey that it would almost overwhelm him. Much later in life, following his retirement, when his wife could not long assist him with daily chores, he would need help. It was suggested that Max try the assistance of a seeing-eye companion, despite his dreadful fear of dogs.

After a month of training, he received Calvin, a chocolate Labrador retriever. Max shared how Calvin had bonded more with his wife and seemed to tolerate him as another part of his job. Calvin could sense Max's distance and fearful reserve daily.

You see, it was during that walk that a car would move into the crosswalk, and Calvin then leaped forward to save Max's life. Son Steve recalls: "Max and Calvin had a green light, so Max gave the command to cross the street. A car coming at them did not slow down, so Calvin abruptly stopped and pulled back to avoid getting hit. Calvin didn't leap in front; they walked side by side, and as the dog stopped and stepped back, Max also did." Max's fear dissolved from that day forward, and Calvin immediately sensed the improvement. For the first time, fear had been replaced by trust, and that would foster a new relationship. Please look for the book written by author Sharon Peters entitled: Trusting Calvin: How a Dog Helped Heal a Holocaust Survivor's Heart.

It was during the Adolf Eichmann trial that a survivor of the Budzyn labor camp named Dr. David Wdowinski in his description of Feiks as Felix in this way:

The commandant Felix told us to stand in two rows. Afterward, he went up to one of the Jews, told him to leave the rank, and ordered him to undress. He then began undressing; he removed his overcoat, and Felix started shouting, "Hurry up – undress completely." This went on until he was altogether naked, drew a revolver, killed this Jew, and said, "This is what will happen to each of you if you do not hand over everything you have, and this is only an example." He demanded gold, silver, good clothes, suitcases, and so on. On the same day, he saw a man of advanced age, an old man, and his first words were, "You old dog – are you still alive?" He ordered the Ukrainians to shoot him and kill him, and he went off.

Then we surrounded the old man, and the Ukrainians could not find him. The commandant came back to the camp half an hour or an hour later and saw the old man – he drew his revolver and shot him. He was a top-rated doctor from Warsaw, very much loved by the Jews of Warsaw – by Dr. Pupko. He was well known, firstly because he was an Orthodox Jew. He prayed every day with his phylacteries and prayer shawl. He would not write any prescriptions on the Sabbath, and apart from that, he was known and loved, for he had done a great deal as a doctor for the poor Jews and had attended to them without payment.

I then took the opportunity to ask Max about the spiritual condition of the prisoners. The question I presented to him was, was there anyone still praying during that time? He replied there were some, but the prayers of the faithful were prayers of lament. The reality was Commander Feiks had the power of life and death. Max recalls one of the faithful that could recite prayers by memory. He was asked about giving thanks while having to endure the hell of oppression, to which the faithful man replied I'm thankful that God created me a Jew and not a murderous Nazi.

In May 1944, as the Soviet army began approaching the Lublin district, the factory installations and some of the workforces were transferred to the salt mines in Wieliczka. Other prisoners from the Budzyn were being moved to surrounding camps such as Skarzysko-Kamienna, Starachowice, Mielec, Ostrowiec, and Majdanek. Max and his brother would be transferred to another aircraft factory at the Flossenbürg concentration camp. He would survive a death march from Flossenbürg and be liberated by American troops. Max recalls the date as April 23, 1945, but most historical records have April 29, 1945.

In review, Max and his brother were sent to the Budzyn labor camp as 1 out of 500 Jews selected from nearby towns and villages; others were either exterminated or sent to the fast-track of the "death camps." Budzyn was at its peak with slightly over 3000 people a few months later, yet Max and his brother were never split-up. Also, Budzyn was a sub-camp of the "death camp" Majdanek, and yet they were both exported to Flossenbürg in 1944 until the end of the war in 1945. Remember these stats? August 1943, 200 of the camp's prisoners were sent to the death camp of Majdanek. Budzyn was declared a concentration camp on October 22, 1943, and on February 8, 1944, scores of prisoners were massacred by Ukrainian guards who were the most brutal of all to the Jews. What was that- "Ukrainian guards who were the most brutal of all to the Jews." This seems like a keynote to bring up some people in the same camps as Max and his brother.

John Demjanjuk was a Ukrainian-American who changed his first name from Ivan to John and moved to the Cleveland suburb of Seven Hills following World War II to become an autoworker. Mr. Demjanjuk was stripped of his US citizenship in 1981 and deported to Israel when he was thought to be the sadist guard, "Ivan the Terrible." He was then a victim of mistaken identity when a photograph on a duty card turned up bearing a striking resemblance.

He was placed on trial, convicted in 1988 in Israel of crimes against humanity, and sentenced to be hanged. The Israeli Supreme Court overturned the conviction five years later when new evidence showed that another Ukrainian was probably the notorious Ivan.

John Demjanjuk regained his US citizenship, only to revoke it under new allegations. He was convicted in 2011 for war crimes (a term internationally accepted and listed by description as an accessory to the murder of 27,900 Jews while acting as a guard at the Sobibor Poland Nazi German extermination camp. and also found to be a volunteer at Flossenbürg, Trawniki, Majdanek, and Okzow.

Since his appeal was pending at his death, John (Ivan) Demjanjuk remains presumed innocent under German law, and his earlier conviction is invalidated. According to the Munich state court, he does not have a criminal record. John (Ivan) Demjanjuk was buried at an "undisclosed location" in the United States.

What did the Ukrainians think of all this, you might ask yourself? On September 22, 2009, the Lviv Regional appealed to the President of Ukraine Viktor Yushchenko, and Prime Minister Yulia Tymoshenko, with Ukraine's parliament to intercede on behalf of John (Ivan) Demjanjuk. The Ukrainian government called the prosecution of John (Ivan) Demjanjuk an "international conspiracy aimed at discrediting Ukraine and Ukrainians in the eyes of world public opinion"; "Without a doubt, the materials of the case were forged and fabricated by KGB."

On a less somber note, I must confess the first time I saw a photo of Flossenbürg, I thought to myself, what a beautiful place to visit. The pines of the Bavarian Forest surrounded it; a small picturesque mining village nestled high in the mountains. If it were anything other than a concentration camp, it would surely be a most desirable place for leisure. Not the case during this segment of history, and stained forever by its going forward.

Flossenbürg was established in May 1938 as a relatively small concentration camp located near the Czech border in northeastern Bavaria. It was a rock quarry where the inmates mined granite. By the time the camp expanded to capacity near the end of the war (when Max and his brother arrived), it had approximately 94,200 prisoners.

In addition to German prisoners, inmates included Russian, Polish, French, Czech, Italian, Greek, Danish, Norwegian, British, Canadian, American nationals, and Jews. Some Allied prisoners of war (POWs), deserters from the German Armed Forces, and common criminals.

Max and many other prisoners at Flossenbürg were employed at the Messerschmitt airplane factory established within the camp in 1942. American forces liberated the camp on April 23, 1945. An estimated 30,000 inmates perished throughout the camp's history. The camp was managed by members of the Schutzstaffel (SS). Originally the elite bodyguards of Adolf Hitler, the SS evolved under Heinrich Himmler into an enormous organization operating in all areas of the Third Reich. SS units served as security police, fought as frontline combat troops, and used the concentration camp system.

The Flossenbürg records showed three classes of prisoners at the camp: prisoners of war (primarily Russian but also including some French, British, Canadian, and American POWs), Jews (Polish and Hungarian), and political prisoners (French, Belgian, Italian, and Yugoslavian).

The camp's records covered primarily October 7, 1943–April 9, 1945. There were noticeable changes in the subtraction lists which provided the prisoner's number, full name, and date of birth. Most commonly, the subtractions were due to death. A fellow survivor that followed much the same trail as our friend Max Edelman is Jack Adelstein (by birth known as Janek Eidelstein).

On April 15, 1936, Jack Adelstein was born to Mordechai and Gertrude Eidelstein as the fifth of six children. His family hid in a cave in a dense forest outside Krasnik, Poland, for six months before the Krasnik ghetto. At Budzyn, Jack recalls being given a uniform he described as "ten times too big" and was assigned to a barracks with his father and brother.

Jack attested to his time at Budzyn (being much younger than Max) in this way:

He stayed in the kitchen during the days, hiding under piles of potato peelings. "I was afraid Felix (Commander Feiks) would see me and kill me," he said of the Oberscharfuhrer (Nazi overseer), Reinhold Felix, who was, according to Jack, "the devil himself."

Felix rode on his white horse at roll call with a German shepherd at his side. Sometimes at night or on weekends, when he was drunk, he walked into a barracks with a small machine gun and sprayed bullets. At those times, Jack's father hid him under a straw mattress.

After three months, Jack was assigned a job feeding chickens, rabbits, and geese. He also had to report to Felix at roll call. One day, in front of 10,000 prisoners, "out of nowhere," Jack said, Felix drew his revolver, cocked it, and pointed it at Jack's head. It jammed. But Felix, enraged by the malfunction, began beating Jack's head with the gun, creating a gash "two fingers" deep. Jack bears a 3-inch scar to this day.

But Jack had already reached a point where "it didn't matter anymore," he remembers. Also, he and his father had heard that Gertrude and the three girls had been taken to Auschwitz. His brother and sister had been murdered, taken to a large ditch outside the camp with a group of 500 prisoners, and shot. And on the camp's row of gallows, "At least 10 to 50 people were hanging every day — by the neck, the feet, and every which way." After six months, Jack and his father were transferred to Flossenbürg, which was "cold as hell." While his father worked on planes for Messerschmitt AG, Jack was assigned to clean the Nazi offices. He recalls stealing bread and cheese for his father to eat with the watery soup they were given once a day.

The camp became unmanageably overcrowded, and the crematorium, working round the clock, could not keep pace. The Nazis piled bodies in stacks, sometimes 20 feet high, pouring gasoline on them and igniting them. When the Allies began bombing in January 1945, the Germans loaded the prisoners on trains. Jack and his father were put in a cattle car, but Jack's father feared the train might also be bombed, so standing on dead bodies, he pulled himself up to the car's roof and climbed out. He then hauled Jack up with him.

As the train was departing and they jumped off, Jack was

shot in the foot. They escaped into the nearby woods but were soon captured and returned to Flossenbürg a few weeks before liberation. There was no food, and thousands of prisoners walked around, "skeletons with their eyes bulging," Jack said. Jack, at age nine, was believed to be the camp's youngest survivor.

US Army Colonel John R. Dabrowski describes the escalation near the end of the war in this way:

While Flossenbürg was not as well-known as the camps of Dachau, Treblinka, and Auschwitz, it was nonetheless a vital part of the Nazis' "Final Solution." in the East, the steamrolling Red Army overran the first of the death camps in Poland in July 1944, starting with Majdanek, near Lublin. Yet, surprisingly, many in the West remained skeptical, dismissing Russian eyewitness accounts and photographs of the camp as "Soviet propaganda."

At Flossenbürg camp, members of the German Resistance to Hitler (and the plot to kill Hitler on July 20, 1944) were executed on the orders of Reichsfuhrer S.S. Heinrich Himmler on April 9, 1945 - just a short time before the camp's liberation. Max confirms that persons of special status as political prisoners were Lutheran Pastor Dietrich

Bonhoeffer, Admiral Wilhelm Canaris (head of the German military intelligence), and Major General Hans Oster. (Photos of each of the men included).

<u>Admiral Wilhelm Canaris</u>

<u>Major General Hans Oster</u>

Pastor Dietrich Bonhoeffer

Bibliography

(http://www.nytimes.com/1993/07/30/world/acquittal-jerusalem-israel-court-sets-demjanjuk-free-but-he-now-without-country.html?pagewanted=all&src=pm;

http://www.president.gov.ua/; and

http://www.bbc.com/news/world-europe-15249184).

https://en.wikipedia.org/wiki/List_of_war_crimes)

(https://en.wikipedia.org/wiki/Sobib%C3%B3r_extermination_camp)

http://news.bbc.co.uk/2/hi/65urope/4035789.stm;

(Kuropas, Myron B.; Shust, Maria; Pevna, Chrystyna (1984). To Preserve a Heritage: The Story of the Ukrainian Immigration in the United States. New York: The Ukrainian Museum. 84-050811. Magocsi, Paul R., ed. (1979), The Ukrainian Experience in the United States: A Symposium, Sources and Documents, Cambridge, Mass.: Harvard Ukrainian Research Institute, ISBN 0-916458-04-0)

Frances Jane Crosby, born March 24, 1820, in Putnam County, New York, and died February 12, 1915, in

Bridgeport, Connecticut. Blinded by an incompetent doctor at six weeks of age,

Frances Jane - Hymns and Carols of Christmas.

https://www.hymnsandcarolsofchristmas.com/Hymns_and_Carols/Biographies/Fanny_Crosby.htm

All prisoners returned for a meal consisting of cabbage soup and a quarter pound of bread by evening. Following the evening meal, the prisoners went to their bunks, numbered five above one another. Although they had no blankets, there were so many in each barrack that their body heat was warm enough.

Budzyn   Labour   Camp
www.HolocaustResearchProject.org.

http://www.holocaustresearchproject.org/ar/labour%20camps/Budzyn/budzyn.html

Please look for the book written by author Sharon Peters entitled: Trusting Calvin: How a Dog Helped Heal a Holocaust Survivor's Heart.

Trusting Calvin: How a Dog Helped Heal a Holocaust

https://fcbookclubkit.wordpress.com/2016/01/27/trusting-calvin-how-a-dog-helped-heal-a-holocausts-survivors-heart/

The commandant Felix told us to stand in two rows.

Budzyn - death camps.

http://deathcamps.org/occupation/budzyn.html

The Israeli Supreme Court overturned the conviction five years later

Justice and his lasting horror - Jewish World Review.

https://www.jewishworldreview.com/0210/Russian_remembers.php3

ACQUITTAL IN JERUSALEM ACQUITTAL IN JERUSALEM; Israel Court Sets Demjanjuk Free, But He Is Now Without a Country By CHRIS HEDGES; Published: July 30, 1993).

ACQUITTAL IN JERUSALEM; Israel Court ... - The New York Times

https://www.nytimes.com/1993/07/30/world/acquittal-jerusalem-israel-court-sets-demjanjuk-free-but-he-now-without-country.html

(War crimes) as an accessory to the murder of 27,900 Jews while acting as a guard

John Demjanjuk.

https://www.liquisearch.com/john_demjanjuk

adopted an appeal to the President of Ukraine Viktor Yushchenko, a

John Demjanjuk | Segunda Guerra Mundial Wiki | Fandom.

https://segundaguerramundial.fandom.com/pt-br/wiki/John_Demjanjuk

In addition to German prisoners, inmates included Russian, Polish, French, Czech, Italian, Greek, Danish, Norwegian, British, Canadian, American nationals, and Jews of all nationalities. Some Allied prisoners of war (POWs), deserters from the German Armed Forces,

Publication Number: M1935 Publication Title: Concentration

https://www.archives.gov/files/research/captured-german-records/microfilm/m1935.pdf

A fellow survivor that followed much the same trail as our friend Max Edelman is Jack Adelstein (by birth known as Janek Eidelstein).

Survivor: Jack Adelstein - Jewish Journal.

https://jewishjournal.com/mobile_20111212/103443/

US Army Colonel John R. Dabrowski describes the escalation near the end of the war in this way:

U.S. Army Liberates Flossenburg Concentration Camp

https://www.army.mil/article/8441/u_s_army_liberates_flos senburg_concentration_camp

ACQUITTAL IN JERUSALEM ACQUITTAL IN JERUSALEM; Israel Court Sets Demjanjuk Free, But He Is Now Without a Country by CHRIS HEDGES; Published: July 30, 1993). https://www.nytimes.com/1993/07/30/world/acquittal-jerusalem-israel-court-sets-demjanjuk-free-but-he-now-without-country.html?pagewanted=all&src=pm

List of war crimes)

(Sobibor extermination camp)

(John Demjanjuk; Amy Knight, The KGB: Police and Politics in the Soviet Union, Unwin Hyman (1990) ISBN 0-04-445718-9;

http://news.bbc.co.uk/2/hi/29urope/4035789.stm;

Офіційне інтернет-представництво Президента України; and http://www.bbc.com/news/world-europe-15249184).

(https://en.wikipedia.org/wiki/John_Demjanjuk; Amy Knight, The KGB: Police and Politics in the Soviet Union, Unwin Hyman (1990) ISBN 0-04-445718-9;

Chapter Three

<u>LiliRussell-Vatican</u>

Guardian Angels: My
Brother's Keeper

"Guardian angels don't always have wings" A guardian angel is allotted the right to protect and guide a particular person, group, or nation. The belief in tese beings can be traced throughout all ancient times. The concept of angels guarding people played a significant role in Ancient Judaism. In the 5th century, the Christianity hierarchy of angels was widely developed by Pseudo-Dionysius the Areopagite.

We all need guardian angels by our side, especially in moments of great despair. They come in many forms and give us hope when we need it the most

"The most devastating day for me in the concentration camp, in fact in my entire life, was April 8, 1944," Max recalls. Two camp guards in Budzyn roughed me up severely and left me for dead. I was a bloody mess. My brother ran to fetch Dr. Forster, a fellow inmate and a good friend. "The Herr Doctor," known to most of us, had been a practicing physician in Austria until the Anschluss. Dr. Forster cleaned me up and applied a cold compress. Then I heard him say to my brother, "He is young, and he will mend. I am worried about his eyes. The left looks bad, and the right could be injured too."

The eyesight that remained in his right eye would begin to deteriorate within the next few months, and he would no longer recognize objects. This made it very difficult to work, and it would become precarious for those around him. Max and his brother realized that sooner or later, they would have to tell Eric, the barracks supervisor, about his blindness. Max said, "That was the longest day of my life."

"You see," said Max, "Eric was a German national political prisoner - "a gentile," and it was his job to report Max as not being able to work. Much to the surprise of Max and his brother, Eric instructed Max to hide above the top bunk in the mornings, saying, 'No one would come here, and you will be safe.' "Eric was a German," Max described, "and the camp officers and guards trusted him." He even warned the inmates in the barracks not to harm or steal food from Max. Eric chose to disregard the consequences of sheltering a blind Jewish prisoner.

Somehow, he managed to see past all the propaganda to discover genuine value in this young Jewish man - even at the risk of his own life. Max looks back on the situation and calls Eric his "guardian angel." Max adopted the phrase while telling his story in an elementary school in the US. Max recalled during our conversation that a little girl raised her hand to speak and likened Eric's assistance to the Christian concept of being a "guardian angel."

However, Max's son Steve makes an important observation about the context in this way: Max often referred to Eric as his guardian angel in his speeches and presentations, but you should be aware that he meant this symbolically rather than literally. Jews believe in angelic spirits but not in angels as personal guardians in the same sense as many Christians do.

It was Sunday, April 15, 1945, and Max's brother would share the news of President Roosevelt's death. The war seemed to be drawing closer to an end, and it was time to leave the Budzyn camp as the Russians drew closer. Meanwhile, at the Flossenbürg camp, everyone was on alert. Max recalls, "We were counted and recounted." Finally, they were lined up in five rows at dawn, and all 2,500 Jews began the "death march." Max held on to his brother's arm on one side and his friend Shlomo's arm on the other. "They marched slowly at first, not knowing where they were going. A steady rain followed and added to our misery."

Max recalls a point when he was ready to give up. He wasn't any hungrier or more exhausted than the others, but the ill-fitting shoes he was forced to wear were more than he could bear. Max mentioned this to his brother and his friend. His friend Shlomo said, "Do you know what day today is?" "Today is April 20, and it's Hitler's birthday. Will you give him your life as a birthday present on this day?" Max's brother offered him his shoes, but Max refused. His brother (standing just inches from an SS guard) mustered the courage to ask if he could take the boots off of a dead man lying on the side of the road. Much to their surprise, the guard gave his permission.

The prisoners were frozen like statues without expression as they marched onward. Then Max said an airplane flew overhead and began dropping leaflets. The guards picked them up - "as we were not allowed." Shortly afterward, the guards disappeared like a vapor into the woods with their machine guns and vicious dogs. "It was an indescribable feeling that day. We were fearful and hopeful simultaneously, and we weren't sure if it was real or just another cruel joke.

As they drew closer to the highway, the sounds of heavy vehicles increased. Everyone could hear as someone shouted, "It's the Americans; we are free!" It was not until that moment did, they dare to believe it to be true. Some were laughing, others crying, and others were just too numb to express any emotion." The Americans provided food from their vehicles as they stopped along the roadside.

Max wasn't feeling well at that point and remembered his brother walking him to a bench nearby a farmhouse where they sought help from an American officer. In perfect German, the American told the woman at the farmhouse to let me in (and several other sick survivors) and make us comfortable.

It was now the morning of the first day of Max's freedom, and he had become keenly aware of his disability for the first time.

He was utterly overwhelmed with self-pity and said to himself, "I am liberated all right, but I am blind, and except for my brother, my whole family has perished. I was practically alone." Max describes it this way: The door opened, and I heard my brother saying, "You have company." Immediately, I was embraced with a big bear hug- it was Eric. "We made it." he explained, "We have survived, and we are free!"

Then Eric noticed that Max was crying.

"Aye, you are crying. Are you in pain?" He inquired.

Max replied as he sobbed, "I have survived, and if it were not for the two of you, I would have gone up in smoke long ago. I am liberated but cannot see my liberators or those rejoicing. I am terrified, and the two of you have done everything possible to keep me away from the oven. Right now, I don't know whether to thank you or not."

The following day, an American officer took Max to a convalescent hospital in Amberg, Bavaria. A nurse took Max to Dr. Hasselt, the only eye doctor in Amberg. (The doctor was a German, of course). He examined his eyes for a brief moment and then said: "Max, you will never see again." Max couldn't believe what he was hearing. He turned to the nurse standing nearby and said, "What else can you expect from a Nazi doctor!"

Unwilling to accept the diagnosis, Max asked to be taken to Munich. He was examined by a specialist named Dr. Meisner, a high-ranking Nazi officer. Max was admitted to the hospital, and they operated on his left eye within two days. The eye cavity was cleaned, and Max was fitted with an artificial eye. Medication therapy soon followed in the right look to revive the optic nerve.

However, after two months of treatment, nothing else could be done to restore sight. The doctor explained that the partial view could have been corrected immediately if treatment had been available. Dr. Meisner advised Max's brother to take him home and return for a follow-up in December. Soon after leaving the hospital, Max fell into depression and said even the landlady of their apartment tried to snap him out of it. Mrs. Eichenmueller knew of a blind music teacher and arranged for Max to meet him. He tried to teach Max to play the violin and the accordion, but all the efforts to encourage him seemed to make him more depressed. The loss of sight was apparent, but Max had also contracted typhus in the camp and suffered from hearing loss due to the fever.

December finally arrived, and Max and his brother returned to Munich for follow-up as advised. When they arrived, they found that Dr. Wesseli had replaced Dr. Meisner. Dr. Wesseli had been head of the clinic before the Nazis gained power, but private physicians who refused to join the Nazis were sent to prison before the war. After a thorough examination, Dr. Wesseli confirmed the prior diagnosis, adding there was nothing medically available to restore Max's eyesight.

Max then explained how this doctor's approach was much different. He asked directly, what do you know about being blind, and what do you intend to do about it? As Max searched his heart in desperation, he replied: "I know nothing about being blind. I recall seeing a woman in our town that was blind, and she would beg the streets..."

The doctor then gave him three options: Doing nothing and becoming a burden to his brother and society. Two, since the Nazis weren't successful in killing him, or three, rebuilding his shattered life in the beginning. "This no-nonsense analysis came again from a stranger, and Max said a German whom I still considered an enemy so soon after the liberation. He was a kind person who earned my trust. We decided on the third option."

He then enrolled in the Rehabilitation School for the Adult Blind in Bavaria and learned to live independently. He had to re-learn many elementary things, like using a knife and fork, shaving, and walking around on his own safely.

He even learned a new form of communication by typing in Braille. The most crucial thing Max learned was a life skill and how to earn wages from his God-given talents and abilities. At twenty-two years old, Max began to live again in a chaotic uncaring world. The scars, however, would remain, and the nightmares continued undiminished.

It was now January of 1946, and Max began his training. He recalls the school was located in Tegernsee, a small lakeside resort town about 45 miles south of Munich.

It was a residential school, and the students lived on campus. There were 70 students, 69 former Nazi officers and soldiers, and myself. The enlisted men differed from the officers as they took their responsibilities as ordinary men and waited for the war to end.

Max chose to study physical therapy and describes the format in this fashion. There were no Talking Books in those days. Most of the textbooks were in Braille or print, and someone had to read them to us. The schedule was deliberate, so there wasn't much time to feel sorry for ourselves. Every Saturday and Sunday afternoon, young ladies from the town nearby volunteered to assist us with recreation. They would take us to a movie or concert or just for a walk to a cafe for coffee and cake. They also read the printed homework so we could study.

Vacations were usually two weeks in the summer and ten days around Christmas and New Year. The school days were long, and the work was hard, eventually paying off. Max would graduate with a diploma in physical therapy and pass the state board examinations in August of 1948.

He found his first job at the Bogenhausen Hospital in Munich on September 1, 1948. He recalls how much he enjoyed working there and wished to have framed his first paycheck.

My wife and I were both very anxious to hear the story of how Max came to meet Barbara, who was a young German Catholic woman working at the hospital, and how she would later become his bride. However, in his modesty, he added, "She decided to take a chance on me."

Upon meeting Barbara's parents, Max explained how he didn't have any family and he was disabled. They seemed more than willing to overlook all of that, assuring him that they were accustomed to those things, as Barbara's father walked with a limp.

It wasn't until later while researching Max's story, I would learn how the Nuremberg Laws had outlawed Jewish Germans from marrying non-Jews. (Max added towards the end of his story that his brother had also married a German woman).

I was more interested in the attraction phase, as it is uncommon for most people to get past an enemy barrier.

As a high school student, I recall how my father would hold a grudge when I shared that I had applied to become a foreign exchange student in Japan. He responded sharply, "I won't have it!" (He was drafted in World War II on the Pacific side to fight the Japanese)

Max and Barbara were married for 53 years, and together raised and educated two sons and have five grandchildren. Sadly, on January 3, 2004, Barbara Edelman passed away after a long illness. During the late 1940s, Max and Barbara came to the United States. Max said, "The nightmares continued unrelentingly, and Barbara and I decided to immigrate to America. We arrived in December of 1951."

Not knowing English and being blind, finding a job would be most challenging. "We decided to put English on the fast track," Max said. While taking classes, a librarian was able to order The English Braille Pocket Dictionary with just seven volumes." (To this day, Max still has every book but has yet to purchase trousers with pockets large enough to hold even one.)

As a gift for Max's testimony, my wife and I got him a

complete Old and New Testament Bible in grade 2 Braille. Much to our surprise, it was shipped in 3 boxes with 17 volumes.

One day Barbara noticed an ad for a masseur at a local health club; Max decided to try it. Max and Barbara went to the health club and applied for the job. After Max introduced himself to the manager and answered a few questions, the manager conveyed that another person was also applying for the job.

The manager said she would notify him once she had made her decision. She then put a folded piece of paper in Max's hand, and on the way out, Barbara told him it was a five-dollar bill. Max was offended, humiliated, and furious.

He returned to the office in broken English (mainly in German); he told the manager he hadn't come for charity but a job. Then he put the five-dollar bill on her desk and walked out.

Max recalls meeting a mobility instructor named Jim from the Cleveland Sight Center who taught him how to use a white-tipped cane. Jim was also blind and knew the streets of Cleveland very well. "Jim was a chain smoker and always had a cigarette in his hand or mouth. He was taller than I and got too close to me with his cigarette one day. Suddenly I smelled something burning, but I didn't say anything.

When I went home, Barbara asked who had burned a hole in my hat. (It was an expensive hat that Max had brought from Germany, and it was ruined). I never mentioned that incident to Jim."

Then an opening became available at Mount Sinai Hospital for a physical therapist. Max said he took his diploma and the letters of recommendation (all German) with him to the interview. As it turned out, the Personnel Director was fluent in German. When she finished reading the documents, she commented on Max's qualifications for the job. However, the department supervisor would agree that Max could be hired.

The director introduced Max to the supervisor and explained his qualifications in detail. The supervisor snipped, "I don't care how qualified he is; I don't want a blind man in my department," and stormed out of the office. Another disappointing blow to Max "And this was supposed to be America, the land of opportunity," Max thought to himself. "Not since the Holocaust had I felt so humiliated. It was perhaps a good thing my wife and I didn't have enough money, or we might have considered returning to Germany." After a short while, Max describes how his language skills had improved, and he was ready to tackle another job perspective.

There was an opening for an X-ray darkroom technician at the Veterans Hospital in Cleveland, but he wasn't eligible for a civil service test. That position was offered to a visually impaired man who worked at the Cleveland Clinic, and the job he was leaving created an open door for Max. Max was introduced to Dr. Hughes, the head of the X-ray department at the Cleveland Clinic. Max describes how he had "two strikes against me because I was blind and a Jew." Then he added how there wasn't any Jewish staff in the X-ray department then. Dr. Hughes had made his decision, and with it, stipulations followed.

However, they were willing to give Max at least a chance to prove himself this time. Dr. Hughes insisted on a six-month probation period (usually standard ninety days).

On top of that, Dr. Hughes was only willing to offer a dollar an hour-salary. That was on October 20, 1952, and the rest is history, as Max would later retire as a physical therapist.

Max recalls his first day on the job at the Cleveland Clinic in this manner: I was greeted by a fellow employee. One man named Art had been employed for six years at that time and took the opportunity to define the boundaries as he had seen them. He abruptly asks Max, "You are a Jew, right? Then he lowered the boom, "We here don't like Jews and don't like niggers, got it?" By that time, Max understood English enough to answer assuredly.

Max had already been advised, "When you get a job, you have to make an extra effort to hold onto it. Work harder than your sighted co-workers; do a better job than they do; don't ever be late to work if you can help it; don't leave until your work is done; even if it takes extra time to finish what you have been doing, and show loyalty to your employer." Of course, that piece of advice came with a tag: "if you practice all these things, the employer might come to consider you a good employee, but never an excellent one."

Max took the advice to heart and determined never to allow his supervisor to question his job performance. Within six months, he had already seen his first obstacle removed. A co-worker named Art had been fired for negligence. Max had shown to be "handicapable" (instead of handicapped), and Dr. Hughes was so impressed he wanted to hire another blind man to replace Art. It wasn't long until the word got out that Max was a physical therapist, and before he knew it, his customer base was quickly growing.

However, the housing market was not where he and Barbara could ultimately settle down. Max recalled an event where he inquired about an apartment from a Christian fundamentalist. Max and Barbara responded to an apartment ad, and when they arrived to check it out, the landlord asked them 'if they were saved.' Max was confused but knew it must have something to do with religion. To which he responded, "We are Jewish." To that, the landlord replied, "No apartment." By this time, Max was getting wise to this game and decided not to go to the next apartment showing but instead allowed Barbara to go. Max would show up after the lease had been signed and not give them any reason to question his integrity going forward.

Finally, Max thought, "an end to all my humiliating experiences..." only to find an incident nearly costing him his job. Inside an x-ray, the darkroom is a viewing box with a bright fluorescent light enabling the technician to see the exposed film briefly. Max recalls one day when the switch had broken. A maintenance electrician had been called to replace it and did so miserably. You see, the switch, when appropriately installed, should be in the down position to indicate the 'offsetting. However, the maintenance electrician had installed the switch upside down. This mistake caused three film cases to be unnecessarily exposed and three patients to return for new x-rays. Once again, Max could hear his accusers say, "It was that blind Jew...."

Max may not have known (and I learned three years after our conversations) that in 1929 The Cleveland Clinic experienced a similar incident dubbed the third worst disaster in Cleveland's history. Don't miss the last sentence of this historical account: The original home of the Cleveland Clinic was not a hospital with beds but a clinic with four stories of doctor's offices surrounding a small central atrium. It is an unassuming 'fireproof' brick building on the south side of Euclid Avenue at East 93rd Street.

Although it is almost lost in the expansive urban landscape, it is the site of one of Cleveland's worst disasters, with the final casualties of 123 dead, including one of the Cleveland Clinic founders, Dr. John Phillips, and 92 injured. It ranks third among Cleveland's Worst Disasters behind the "Collinwood School Fire" and the "East Ohio Gas Explosion." The disaster was triggered when an x-ray film came too close to a light bulb.

Max thought the worst after years of experiencing bigotry and hatred but tried to give his supervisors the benefit of the doubt. Indeed, they did prove to be the reason men that he had assured himself they were. Max had established a reputation as a reliable and loyal employee and was now beginning to be treated that way as his persistence was paying off. When he travels to speak, Max is often asked how he survived in a Nazi concentration camp when thousands were dying every day, and you were a blind man.

Max often comments that the most straightforward answer might be "by the grace of God" but quickly retracts that as "too simplistic a response." Then he recalled a young school-aged girl named Sarah saying to him; there is no doubt you had a guardian angel, and the Lord saved you for this purpose.

To this, she implied that people like his brother, Eric, and the German doctor might have been just that. Max affirmed guardian angels and friends who genuinely are their brother's keeper.

Max said he often recalls when Eric read to him from the German philosopher Freidrich Nietzsche who said: What does not destroy me makes me stronger. (Maxims and

Arrows, 8)

Max concludes that I have remembered that quotation whenever I have felt humiliated and degraded as a blind person during the past sixty years. The Max Edelman story is one of incredible resiliency and grace. Then to come to the foreign land of your liberators, only to find hatred and bigotry still existed. How difficult it must have been to try and remain a silhouette weaving about, masquerading as "normal" in an abnormal environment.

Max Edelman is an overcomer who developed a 'fighter's spirit.' Call him blessed to be surrounded by people who love and encourage him to excel. Max has learned to balance goodness and mercy and now declares with his lips: "Hate is the acid that corrodes the soul." As long as there have been ancient tales of human endurance, we have been intrigued with people who overcome adversity and succeed in life.

We have all pondered the differences at one point. What makes one life different from another, and can those positive influences be fostered? Is there some kind of magic in life that is more than just ordinary, which makes resilient people stand out?

I'm confident that magic has nothing to do with it and that

godly character will take you far. Undeniably, we will all have to deal with life's complex realities. Those challenging surprises when we allow our guard to slip that knock the wind out of us with a blowing jab. The things we didn't factor in can change everything in less than a nanosecond. Our reactions to the unexpected things in life reflect our resiliency or lack thereof. People often live on the edge of life, having survival concepts based on fear. We should never allow the circumstances of life to lead us just because we feel they are out of our control.

From a Christian perspective, the Apostle Paul offers two approaches to circumstances that seem out of our control. At one point, he says the situation may depend upon you making personal changes.

In the New Testament book of Romans 12:2, he writes: "Do not conform to the pattern of this world but be transformed by renewing your mind. Then you will be able to test and approve what God's will is—his good, pleasing and perfect will." Then, on the other hand, he seems to acknowledge that there are situations where you have done everything we know to stand, and it's just a matter of maintaining your ground. In the New Testament book of Ephesians 6:13, he says, "Therefore put on the full armor of God, so that when the day of evil comes, you may be able to stand your ground, and after you have done everything, to stand."

My grandmother had a detached retina early in my career as an Optician, and I recall making her a pair of rose-colored glasses. Too often, we view life through filters that shade our perception of reality. That tired old phrase that says "experience is the best teacher" is one of those lenses. Thinking of this nature will create a reality of fear that paralyzes us in times of crisis. It also makes misconceptions that produce false conclusions. You don't have to experience something to know it is wrong! We have to realize that emotions are not reliable gauges to govern our lives. God gave us emotions to enhance our lives but not be led by them.

In the New Testament book of Ephesians 5:15-16 KJV, the Apostle Paul says, "See then that you walk circumspectly not as fools, but as wise, redeeming the time because the days are evil."

Walking circumspectly means living morally and being mindful of our surroundings and situations. I moved my family from Illinois to Ohio just before the World Trade Center bombing of 911. I remember commenting on how cold people had become towards one another just before that incident and what a radical change there was following.

Being mindful of our situations allows us to shift our circumstances radically. When we live in a state of mindfulness, it minimizes our blind spots.

Let me offer four descriptive ways of building resilience in your lifestyle.

Firstly, try adding more compassion. In areas where you were once judgmental, try being supportive of others. You might find that the fog in your life will begin to clear.

Secondly, be more accepting of others that are not like you. It's easy to accept people who are just like you, but it's the differences that make us uncomfortable. Sometimes having the strength to move outside our comfort zone helps us distinguish reality.

Thirdly, foster a lifestyle of openness. Being progressively open with others allows the most difficult situations to become growth opportunities. Honesty is more than just being transparent; it will enable people to grow without overriding their will.

Finally, you must allow for an avenue of creativity. There are times in life when we just can't-do it the way it has always been. It's going to have to be a new thing. We can work and pray with an excellent vision for things to get better without being fixated on our expectations (please take the time to re-read that statement).

Living resiliently is more than just bouncing back; it is about shifting our perceptions, altering our responses, and facing something new with courage.

Most of us are just ordinary people, but what sets us apart is how we respond to the challenges in life. It's the extraordinary possibilities we afford with supernatural wisdom and strength. The courage and emotional stamina we can draw from one another make us resilient. We may not have control over all the events in our lives, but we can control how we respond to those events. Facing each obstacle and walking through it one step at a time makes us resilient people.

Having a sense of personal purpose in life is probably an essential characteristic of resilience. When we determine to keep going forward, despite the roadblocks of failure and rejection, we develop a lifestyle of resiliency. Setting realistic goals and attaining them builds resilient qualities like perseverance.

One day, I considered this illustration while reviewing a wonderful life testimony of a man who bears the name of many of my great fathers but has no relation. He is a rancher in Oregon, and his name is David Noble. When considering purpose and perseverance, I'm often reminded of the dangerous job of a rodeo clown. While the rodeo clown appears to be a comic outside, wearing makeup and traditional costume, he's not just another entertainer.

The rodeo clown is an American bullfighter. He is a skilled athlete with speed, agility, and the ability to anticipate the bull's next move. The rodeo clown has the job of protecting the bull rider from the bull once they have been bucked off (or have jumped off) of the animal. He distracts the bull while making himself a conspicuous target. The rodeo clown's success is never taking his eyes off the bull. Too often, rodeo clowns develop personal idiosyncrasies that cause serious injuries or fatalities.

When people become over-confident and arrogant in their abilities, they take their eyes off the bull and set themselves up for personal failures. My point here is simple and easy to recall: There will be hell to pay if you take your eyes off the bull.

Resilient people learn to laugh at themselves and their circumstances. I'm reminded of a question my wife asked Max Edelman following our interview. She asked him if he had ever watched a popular cooking show on TV. Max quickly took humor in her misuse of words and said: "Stefany... I'm blind, and I don't watch anything!" Then he turned on the console TV in his living room before us and said, "Do you see any picture on that TV? No- and I'm not going to fix it either; because I can hear it just fine".

We can develop problem-solving skills with a clear understanding of your capabilities and limitations. As a young boxer, one quickly learns that if you pound away at your opponent's midsection, sooner or later, he will drop his guard, and you could score a devastating blow to his face.

However, in the 1970s, the world watched a talented boxer named Muhammad Ali perfect technique he called "rope-a-dope." He would throw his body against the ropes as his opponent would wear himself out trying to follow his bouncing frame. Then he would intensely pound away at his opponent until finally landing the fatal blow.

One of the best qualities of resilient people is they have learned to become comfortable with who they are. While we live in a world surrounded by people, we often avoid being alone.

Even life without technology seems to be a deafening silence. Resilient people don't need to be anything but unique and soon discover the value of their worth. They surpass the pressure to conform and realize that they may be called upon to go it alone at any given time.

Throughout my lifetime, I have always admired President Abraham Lincoln. Being born and raised in Illinois with a deep heritage in Kentucky, I have found many things in common. While Abraham Lincoln's lifestyle appears successful, it was riddled with failure after failure. He lost his first love to typhoid, was defeated in eight elections, couldn't get into law school, and even went bankrupt.

Finally, he won the presidential election of 1860 by a split ticket, only to see the country divide and then be shot and killed by an assassin's bullet in 1865. Despite his failures, he will forever be remembered as one of the most outstanding leaders in American history.

My conclusion to this topic is simple: the first thing God wants you to know about life is that you must have a sense of personal identity that causes your heart to surge with strength from within. Living a lifestyle of resiliency is formulated by many qualities birthed out of hardship and tears. If you don't allow mistakes to paralyze you and continue to move forward, you will always find success. God instructed Joshua following Moses' death in Joshua 1:9, "Have I not commanded you? Be strong and courageous. Do not be afraid; do not be discouraged, for the Lord your God will be with you wherever you go." For the Christian, knowing who you are in Christ will take you far above who you could ever become in your human abilities.

Bibliography

The most devastating day for me in the concentration camp, in fact in my entire life, was April 8, 1944,"

Liberation of a Blind Survivor - National Federation of.... https://www.nfb.org/images/nfb/publications/bm/bm04/bm 0405/bm040508.htm

in 1929 The Cleveland Clinic

GC3CEHJ The Cleveland Clinic Fire of 1929 (Traditional .... https://www.geocaching.com/geocache/GC3CEHJ_the-cleveland-clinic-fire-of-1929

Freidrich Nietzsche who said: What does not destroy me makes me stronger.

Jeune Gal - Blogger. https://jeunegal.blogspot.com/

Walking circumspectly means living morally and being mindful of our surroundings

What does it mean to walk circumspectly (Ephesians 5:15 .... https://www.gotquestions.org/walk-circumspectly.html

Living resiliently is more than just bouncing back; it is about shifting our perceptions,

Mindfulness: The Art of Cultivating Resilience. https://psychcentral.com/lib/mindfulness-the-art-of-cultivating-resilience

He lost his first love to typhoid, was defeated in eight elections, couldn't get in

Fall Quarterly Newsletter - Resilience - C20120810-01. http://lifesolutionsforyou.com/pdf/Fall%20Quarterly%20Newsletter%20-%20Resilience.pdf

(Brad Clifton, "The Cleveland Clinic X-Ray Fire of 1929," Cleveland Historical, accessed November 28, 2017, https://clevelandhistorical.org/items/show/573;

https://www.geocaching.com/geocache/GC3CEHJ_the-cleveland-clinic-fire-of-1929)

Do Jews Believe in Guardian Angels?

http://www.chabad.org/library/article_cdo/aid/678751/jewish/Do-we-believe-in-guardian-angels.htm

Chapter Four

Montalcino, Italy

The Need for a Bridge

In Lehman terms, the bridge is inherently symbolic of communication and union. For this reason, it can be seen as the connection between God and Man.

Now whether it be between heaven and earth or even two distinct realms is up to interpretation. It may be a passage to reality or merely a symbol for travel and crossing.

Let me reiterate that the purpose of writing this book is to inspire Christians to become a reflection of Jesus Christ in this life.

As Oswald Chambers, an early-twentieth-century Scottish Baptist evangelist and teacher who was aligned with the Holiness Movement, once said, "The greatest characteristic a Christian can exhibit is this completely unveiled openness before God, which allows that person's life to become a mirror for others.

When the Spirit fills us, we are transformed, and by beholding God, we become mirrors. You can always tell when someone has been beholding the glory of the Lord because your inner spirit senses that he mirrors the Lord's character. Beware of anything that would spot or tarnish that mirror in you."

Have you noticed how couples begin to resemble one another the longer they're married? Well, the same is true of us. It is a matter of fact that the more time we spend in intimate fellowship with Jesus, the more His likeness will be transferred to our lives and surroundings. We cannot change ourselves. If we want to be more like Jesus, we must tend our connection with the Vine.

(John 15:5 New International Version)

"I am the vine; you are the branches. If you remain in me and I in you, you will bear much fruit; apart from me, you can do nothing."

We won't have to manufacture Christ-likeness. If we do, the Fruit of the Spirit will come directly from His work in our lives.

22: But the fruit of the Spirit is love, joy, peace, longsuffering, gentleness, goodness, faith, 23 Meekness, temperance: against such, there is no law.

I like this statement:

We must ask God to give us a genuine curiosity to know other people better. Talk less about yourself and inquire more about them.

It keeps people from becoming "phoney"!

Bad things happen to good people, but it doesn't mean we can check out of life.

Our lives must reflect Him with true resiliency in our identity. We purpose to be happy, and our focal point is destiny. As awkward as that sounds, it is broken down in straightforward strides daily.

Being comfortable with purpose means we are grateful for what we have, becoming a blessing to others. Having a focal point based on destiny is in knowing that God's will for every Christian is to be conformed to the image of Jesus Christ.

Finally, in reflecting Christ with true resiliency in our identity, we become people of courage, and after having done all to stand, we stand firm. (Eph. 6:13)

While I have attempted to stress that these three elements are infused within us by Creator God and are exemplified by His loving-kindness towards us, there remains the need for a bridge. In formulating practical applications, religion often requires a bridge.

In silencing the overtones of the world that screams 'the Church no longer resembles the person of Jesus Christ, there remains the need for a bridge.

Recently, I allowed a fellow Missionary who has been a veteran in the fields of Colombia for 30 years to read and give me constructive feedback on my manuscript. Dr. Dale Meade suggested a bridge from the testimony of Max Edelman to the following chapters that would sharpen the focus of the purpose of writing this book.

The first three chapters of this book focus on and seek to explain the testimony of an innocent teenager who found himself suddenly in captivity by a hostile society just because he was Jewish.

Furthermore, it aims to illustrate how life often brings about wicked unexpected tragedy into our lives, and if we live through those events, we have the option of becoming "bitter" or "better" as a result. If we blame God or others, we cannot be free from the event(s).

I understand from the Bible that even though God's divine plan for your life may include tragedy, it doesn't mean He caused it. He does allow it, but because you lived through it, you are responsible for making society a better place.

Jesus Christ said in John 16:33: "These things I have spoken unto you, that in me ye might have peace. In the world ye shall have tribulation: but be of good cheer; I have overcome the world" (King James Version).

Such is life. It can be tragic and full of tests we think we aren't ready for, but when the time comes, we must face the challenges head-on, for we are the children of God, and he watches over us and tests us so that we never stray the path. Bad things happen to good people, but it doesn't mean we can check out of life. We must go forward, as it benefits us and everyone we encounter.

Like the fourth commandment in honoring the Sabbath, my bridge seeks to solidify heaven and earth, so purpose urges the need for the application. In the vulcanization process in rubber production, there was a missing element in its usefulness for raincoats, boots, tires, and several other things. In Max Edelman's testimony, we see a people forced to be resilient to survive, but were the Hebrews the only people in history to exemplify this quality?

In recent times, we have genocides in Rwanda, Bosnia-

Herzegovina, and Sudan called "ethnic cleansing. "The story of the Hebrew people remains the best example of telling God's story of outreach to humanity because of His binding covenant with them.

One of my favorite stories of survival during modern times is about a small Christian community in one of the remotest corners of Scotland. In the northern archipelago surrounded by the brutal forces of nature amid the Atlantic Ocean is the uninhabited island, St Kilda. No one had lived on St Kilda since 1930 when the last of the 36 residents were evacuated as "hostages of nature."

The island has a 45-degree slope that makes it a haven for seafaring birds to nest and only a gestation period of three months during the summer. In their struggle to survive, the people planted small barley crops, raised sheep, collected eggs from the seafaring birds, and caught puffins (sea parrots) using fishing rods. To capture the eggs from nesting birds, they would climb the jagged cliffs to rob the nests by night. They were indeed a testimony of resiliency in their daily struggle to overcome the forces of nature. While they entertained relocating to the mainland, there was never a "bridge" until all hope was lost. The government realized another generation could not possibly survive on the island.

A bridge helps us cross an insurmountable divide, and it must be built from a starting point with a destiny in mind. It must have purpose and design and be carried out by effort- too often by blood, sweat, and tears. What is it in your life that seems impossible and uncrossable? It may not be the Red Sea, but it can be just as impossible.

God knows there is a need for a bridge in today's world with what is happening all around. Wars, famine, betrayal, and loss of faith, the bridge can mend those divides. If you've ever been misunderstood or misrepresented, you know there's a need for a bridge, for it is through it we can become truly a reflection of Christ as we navigate the current world.

To quote Mathew, "Love God and love your neighbor" These are the six words that should be etched in the heart of every Christian out there. Through the bridge, we can only reach our fellow Christians who have led astray but also to different religions as well.

The bridge is formed by communicating and patiently understanding the thoughts and intentions of others for the simple purpose of reconciliation. 2 Corinthians 5:11-21 tells us that we have been made ambassadors for Christ to reconcile the world to God using the Gospel message as a bridge.

On June 16, 1858, in Springfield, IL, just 30 miles from my hometown of Bloomington-Normal, Abraham Lincoln gave a famous speech saying, "A house divided against itself cannot stand." He was running against Stephen Douglas for the United States Senate. Lincoln's law partner, William Herndon, questioned such a lofty use of words, but Lincoln was paraphrasing the words of Jesus in Mark 3:25. Truth is unstoppable and without borders of time. Its most straightforward application will become a bridge to a golden highway.

This message of reconciliation creates a bridge between God and humanity. In Colossians 1:20-23, Paul explains it this way:

"And through him to reconcile to himself all things, whether things on earth or things in heaven, by making peace through his blood, shed on the cross. Once, you were alienated from God and were enemies in your minds because of your evil behavior. But now he has reconciled you by Christ's physical body through death to present you holy in his sight, without blemish and free from accusation if you continue in your faith, established and firm, not moved from the hope held out in the gospel. This is the gospel you heard and proclaimed to every creature under heaven, and of which I, Paul, have become a servant".

Think about some of the ways we name our bridges today, and you get to find purpose and meaning- sometimes obscure. I found a website with a "bridge name generator" that gives you ten random bridge names based on real-life sources. Give it a try.

In its most fluid use, reconciliation means renewing a friendship or restoring a proper relationship.

Have you ever found a long-lost friend or family member, and by research or social media, re-connected with them? How exciting it is- the discovery is so precious you want the relationship to grow and expand. Jesus boldly proclaimed in John 14:6 that there was no way to God apart from him, and it was complete in him. He said, "I am the way, the truth, and the life; no one comes to the Father but by me." While that statement is problematic and offensive to many people, it is the bridge that God has chosen.

While every Christian has been called to the Ministry of Reconciliation, a few have been chosen to reconcile whole people groups and cultures to the knowledge of Jesus Christ.

If you have been selected for this task, you can be sure that you will be misunderstood and rejected by many even before the job begins.

As a young man, I recall telling my father about starting high school that I felt a call to ministry. His response was a fair one; he said, "that's fine, but Ministers don't make any money. You'll have to learn a trade.'

Since my father died of skin cancer while I was a freshman in high school, I honored his words, learned to make eyeglasses, and then studied the Bible and became a Missionary. Even to this day, my wife restrains me from casting it all aside and moving to the far reaches of the earth in search of the echoes of God's calling. For a Missionary, faith has no boundaries, and where God leads you,

He will always provide for you. If you can dare to believe and trust that God is faithful, he will always show up when you least expect him.

I'm reminded of the story of a young man from a wealthy American family whose mother was faithful to taking him to Church as he grew.

When he graduated high school, his parents gave him the gift

111

of travel- a trip around the world. At that point, he learned firsthand that there were cultures of people groping around in the darkness of sin. He heard the echoes of God's calling to become a bridge and vowed to one day serve them.

He studied at such Ivy League schools as Yale and Princeton, and then upon his ordination in 1912, he set off to Egypt to learn Arabic, and then his destination would be China.

On March 21, he was taken ill with spinal meningitis; nineteen days later, he died on April 9, 1913. He didn't even reach China, where God had called him, but his heart was fixed on the prize. At his death, he gave his inheritance to the cause of reaching people with the good news of the life, death, and burial of Jesus Christ. When he died, they found written in his Bible during three separate segments of his journey: No reserves. No retreat. No regrets. He was born in 1887 in Chicago to the very wealthy Borden family.

Many of you might recall the Borden Dairy Co., known for its mascot, Elsie the Cow. This is the life story of William Whiting Borden, known as Borden of Yale.

I hope the life story of William Borden has inspired you to listen for the echoes of God's calling to become a bridge. I pray it moves you beyond the boundaries of your safety nets where God can prove his faithfulness. In Luke 10: 2, Jesus said to them the harvest is plentiful, but the laborers are few.

Therefore, pray earnestly to the Lord of the harvest to send laborers into his harvest. I recall preaching in the deep jungles of Kalimantan Indonesia (the Dutch called it Borneo) under an open-air pavilion. As the night settled in around us, I looked out into the darkness and saw the steadfast eyes of many of the island's indigenous peoples called the Dayak.

I learned that they were once a warring tribe of headhunters before many were converted to Christianity. Now they are warm and loving people absorbing word after word, applying line after line of God's truth. Isaiah 28:10 says it best: For it is precept upon precept, upon principle, line upon line, line upon line, here a little, there a little. I was probably the only white man for hundreds of miles, and it didn't seem to matter because God had given me what I'll call an Asian heart many years before coming here. I was nothing more than a bridge, yielded and still at the hands of the master builder.

I learned that true happiness came from gratitude and being a conduit of God's love. I never had to decide between the wealth of this world and the riches of heaven, like William Borden. Yet there seemed to be something spun into the deepest parts of my being, much the way the Psalm describes the deep calls to the deep. (Psalm 42:7). It was a quest calling Coming and get me if you dare.

If we want to be more like Jesus, we must keep God at the center of all we do. When He works in and through our lives, let's be sure to give Him credit. When we mess up and fail, let's give Him the broken pieces trusting that He will know how to use it all for His glory. In all things and at all times, be quick to give Him praise.

Bibliography

http://www.fantasynamegenerators.com/bridge-names.php#.WhzfI9Ltzcs

http://www.fantasynamegenerators.com/bridge-names.php#.WhzfI9Ltzcs

every Christian is to be conformed to the image of Jesus Christ.

Romans 8:29 Meaning of Conformed to the Image ... - ConnectUS.

https://connectusfund.org/romans-8-29-meaning-of-conformed-to-the-image-of-his-son

It is my understanding from the Bible that even though God's divine plan for your life

Death and judgement day - WELS.

https://wels.net/faq/death-and-judgement-day/

Jesus Christ said in John 16:33: "These things I have spoken unto you, that in me ye might have peace. In the world ye shall have tribulation: but be of good cheer; I have overcome the world"

(Borden of Yale by Geraldine Taylor; Published May 1, 1988, by Bethany House Publishers- first published November 1926; Original Title: Borden of Yale (Men of Faith).

WHAT THE BIBLE SAYS ABOUT WORRY - I Need A Word.

https://ineedaword.org/what-the-bible-says-about-worry/

ambassadors for Christ to reconcile the world to God

Random Provocations.

https://thesnarkyprophet.blogspot.com/

In Colossians 1:20-23, Paul explains it this way:

"And through him to reconcile to himself all things, whether things on earth or things in heaven, by making peace through his blood, shed on the cross.

Grandy, David. "'in Christ All Things Hold Together': A Christian Perspective (via Levinas And Shimony) On Quantum Entanglement." Dialogue : A Journal of Mormon

Thought, vol. 50, no. 2, Dialogue Foundation, July 2017, p. 87.

Once, you were alienated from God and were enemies in your minds because of your evil behavior. But now he has reconciled you by Christ's physical body through death to present you holy in his sight, without blemish and free from

The Hope Held Out In The Gospel—Colossians 1:21-23.

https://www.jcblog.net/romans/8/65-blog/colossians/colossians-1/694-the-hope-held-out-in-the-gospel-colossians-1-21-23

John 14:6 that there was no way to God apart from him, and it was complete in him. He said, "I am the way, the truth, and the life;

Jeremiah, David. "Pointing Upward." The Triangle Tribune, vol. 21, no. 15, Charlotte Post Publishing Co., 21 July 2019, p. 5A.

On March 21, he was taken ill with spinal meningitis; nineteen days later, he died on April 9, 1913.

Borden of Yale | 5 Minutes in Church History.

https://www.5minutesinchurchhistory.com/borden-of-yale/

the harvest is plentiful, but the laborers are few. Therefore pray earnestly to the Lord of the harvest to send out laborers into his harvest.

Booth, Robbie. "God As The Agent Of Kingdom Growth: An Argument For Divine Passives In Matthew 13:32, 33." Journal of the Evangelical Theological Society, vol. 62, no. 4, Evangelical Theological Society, Dec. 2019, p. 705.

G. Kittel, G. W. Bromiley & G. Friedrich, Ed., Theological Dictionary of the New Testament, Electronic ed. (Grand Rapids, MI: Eerdmans, 1964), 6:175.)

(The Fruit of Spirit needs explanation in this context- the scriptural quote is enough).

Galatians 5:22-23 King James Version:

Chapter Five

The Jester

Happiness Defined

In the dictionary, happiness "means feeling or showing pleasure or contentment" Happiness can be defined in different ways, yet many people have forgotten what that really means.

For me, Mother Teresa explained it best "Profound joy of the heart is like a magnet that indicates the path of life."

Mother Teresa is someone who, during her lifetime, became famous as the Catholic nun who dedicated her life to caring for the destitute and dying in the slums of Calcutta. I will talk about her later in the chapter in more detail.

In the random survey among my friends, I quickly discovered happiness means different things to different people. Before I even start a conversation about happiness, we must first define how happiness is measured. What makes a person, a region, or a country a happy one? After doing research, I found out that these are the factors that define happiness

- Social support
- Life expectancy

- Freedom to make life choices
- Generosity
- GDP per capita
- Perceptions of corruption
- Positive and negative affects

Each of these factors determines how happy people are as a collective. Take Africa, for example. Most nations in the region are miserable because of all the factors mentioned above. They have not had a fair crack at life because of these factors; hence they are low on the happiness index though they are strong people who are religious. For many, their belief in Jesus Christ has helped them survive.

Moving forward European regions, America, and the rest of the west have a high happy index because of how well built their structures are. But even within Europe, there is one country that is the unhappiest. Ukraine ranks in last place, making it the unhappiest country in Europe. Ukraine has experienced ongoing challenges since the Maidan Uprising peaked in 2014.

Events in the country had recently taken a turn for the worse when Russia launched a full-scale invasion of Ukraine on February 24, 2022. As a result of the conflict, over 3 million people have fled the country.

Another factor that is of utmost importance that has really affected happiness is the role of technology. Research shows that technology and social media's advent have made us more depressed and self-conscious. The dopamine in our brains goes into overdrive when we are on social media.

Our phones have entirely taken over our lives and have led to depression, especially in the lives of teens". It's a distraction from the reality facing us every day as it gives us a false sense of happiness through materialism. In a lot of ways, this is an actual test of our patience and belief as we try to navigate through the world. The black screens in front of us have taken over, and we are a slave to them and made them our masters.

Every day we move further away from the glory of God and all because of our temptation. We have made false happiness through our mobile phones and technology, and instead, what we feel is a small dose of dopamine which becomes an addiction like any other drug, and you start to miss its presence so much that other things such as family or friends don't matter as much. Religion also takes a back seat leaving you depressed and alone. This is important to know as many people mistake true happiness for this, and it needs to change.

Moving forward, as I scanned the results online further, I found a summer workshop at an ivy-league university where you could study the Science of Happiness and its practical applications and even get an online certificate for the Psychology and Philosophy of Happiness.

How cool is that? Maybe conveying the meaning of this happiness thing won't be as difficult as I first thought.

However, in light of a thousand different gurus touting remedies to resolve the issues of human misery, it seemed a little obscure to hear the creator of Peanuts, Charles Schulz, with characters saying, "Happiness is a warm puppy."

Speaking of obscurity, let me digress for a moment to interact with a character who defines the topic best, in my opinion. The place was the Cathedral of Saint Mary of the Immaculate Conception, Peoria, Illinois, and the time was December 10, 1995. I was a young Protestant Minister who was one of about 150 non-parish members (general public) allowed inside the Cathedral for this special event. I stood outside on the Cathedral steps with a crowd of an estimated number of between 350 and less than 500. (As a Minister, sometimes we count ears instead of heads.)

As the ushers opened the doors, our hearts were pounding with anticipation, and the crowd began to flow in. We watched intensely as the line inched forward towards the doorway.

The doors were then closed as the church was packed, and the Mass began. There I stood outside in wind chill temperatures near zero degrees Fahrenheit, with a smothering crowd warmed by the spontaneous excitement of our neighbors.

The Mass was about 15 minutes into the session when the usher came to the door again. This time he shouted to the crowd: "We have room for only eight more, and you will have to stand."

Somehow, I was numbered among the eight and found myself following the rest of the crowd to a space on the upper balcony.

During the communion, I walked down to the front of the Cathedral, where I was instructed to cross my arms (like other Protestants) and prepare to receive a blessing. Following the communion, the guest speaker, with her larger-than-life status, stepped forward to offer a prayer to the Virgin Mary and spoke briefly about the mission she had founded some fifty years prior. On that day, seven members of her mission, the Missionaries of Charity (Nuns), would renew their vows.

A calling and commission that would consume their personhood were vows of poverty, chastity, and wholehearted obedience to the service of the poor. It was a lifestyle that these Nuns would consider as the 'lest they could do.'

She had once vowed to live upon the lepers and the poorest of India's Calcutta. She was a beautiful example of a lifestyle of compassion and brokenness, even after worldly fame.

Receiving the Nobel Peace Prize (1979), the Presidential Medal of Freedom (1985 by President Ronald Reagan), and the crowning gem of her life 20 years after her death on September 04, 2016, Pope Francis announced she would be canonized as a Saint.

With a humble voice, she began to quote from Matthew 25: 35, 36 For I was hungry, and you gave me food, I was thirsty, and you gave me drink, I was a stranger, and you made me welcome, lacking clothes and you clothed me, sick and you visited me, in prison and you came to see me.

It was a short delivery but, in my opinion, just as powerful as Abraham Lincoln's Gettysburg Address. Then the Bishop announced that a gift on her behalf would be given to the crowd, and once again, the lines began to form as the gift was circulated. As I got closer to the front, the deacon again instructed the rest of the crowd to prepare themselves for a blessing, as they were all out of medallions. Mother Teresa reached out her small wrinkled hands holding tightly to mine with love and compassion in her eyes as I passed by.

I received her blessing differently because, as a Protestant, she was a servant of God- just like me. I remember telling myself it was just my luck after all my efforts- I had no proof of the experience. Without the medallion, the experience would become just another story anyone could tell. However, the outcome was indeed a happy moment for me. I never shared the event following, because I feared no one would believe it.

I can't say the event changed my life, but I did walk away with a deeper comprehension of the calling of God and the despair of humankind. The selfless obedience to follow a calling to serve the needs of fallen humanity was something the missionary inside of me could relate to. So, like the Virgin Mary following the announcement of Jesus' birth, I, too, pondered this thing in my heart for years to come.

Years later, on June 06, 2018, my wife and I would plan a trip to Italy to celebrate our 29th wedding anniversary. Before our trip to Italy, I decided to share my story about Mother Teresa with the Vatican.

Two weeks later, much to our surprise, a letter from the Vatican Secretary of State arrived in the mail with an autographed photo and an invitation to an audience with Pope Francis. What an incredible event it was! We began the trip in Rome at the Vatican, rented a villa in Tuscany, and drove through the countryside, visiting wineries and 14th and 15th-century villages.

In Florence, we absorbed enough Art/Church history to last a lifetime, and then the grand finale was back to Rome for more museums.

So now, when I quote Mother Teresa's happiness perspective, it has true meaning. Listen as she describes happiness in light of our interaction with others. I see in my mind's eye a time when a little-wrinkled woman, with a tiny hand, spoke words of blessing into my life. I see a smiling Pope (Pope Francis) bridging the gap, and I wonder what unspoken treasures people take to their graves without sharing.

People are often unreasonable and self-centered. Forgive them anyway. If you are kind, people may accuse you of ulterior motives. Be kind anyway. If you are honest, people may cheat you. Be honest anyway. If you find happiness, people may be jealous. Be happy anyway. The good you do today may be forgotten tomorrow. Do well anyway. Give the world the best you have; it may never be enough. Give your best always. For you see, it is between you and God in the end. It was never between you and them anyway.

— Mother Teresa

In 1913 hymn writer Charles A. Miles wrote a song that would forever be an intimate part of my grandmother's Christian experience. As a teenager, I watched as she played the organ and sang the song as though she and Jesus were the only ones in the room. When she died, my aunts attempted to select the music for her funeral, and I recall one aunt saying exacting what everyone else was thinking. She said, "Choose anything but that song, In the Garden." We all understood the happiness it brought her as she imaged the details the hymn writer used to describe Mary as she came to a garden tomb that first Easter morning.

In the book of John 20:15-16, it reads: He asked her, "Woman, why are you crying? Who is it you are looking for?" Thinking he was the gardener, she said, "Sir, if you have carried him away, tell me where you have put him, and I will get him. Jesus said to her, "Mary." She turned toward him and cried out in Aramaic, "Rabboni!" (This means "Teacher"). What an extraordinary moment of happiness for Mary. These contrasts with the moment when Adam and Eve had allowed the poison of sin to forever break their intimate fellowship with Creator God. Genesis 3: 8 says: Then the man and his wife heard the sound of the LORD God as he was walking in the garden in the cool of the day, and they hid from the LORD God among the trees of the garden. Charles A. Miles writes it so well in this hymn:

In The Garden

I come to the garden alone,

while the dew is still on the roses,

and the voice I hear falling on my ear

129

Parson To Person: Three Things God Wants You To Know About Life

The Son of God discloses.

Refrain:

And He walks with me, and He talks with me,

And He tells me I am His own;

and the joy we share as we tarry there,

None other has ever known.

He speaks, and the sound of His voice

is so sweet the birds hush their singing

and the melody that He gave to me

within my heart is ringing.

I'd stay in the garden with Him,

though the night around me be falling,

But He bids me go; through the voice of woe

His voice to me is calling.

In all fairness, the quest for happiness appears in many writings outside of the Judeo-Christian records of Psychological and philosophical essays from China, India, and Greece dating back nearly 2,500 years written by revered men of old. Men such as Confucius, Buddha, Socrates, and Aristotle wrote to their followers about the path of happiness.

Before we look at a few of these characters in detail, let us get a rudimentary (fundamental) definition of happiness. A consensus helps us understand where people come from in their description and use of the word "happiness."

Can we agree that happiness is a mental and emotional state of mind based on outward circumstances? If so, let us take a step further by distinguishing its mean in two different facets. We'll call those two facets: Pleasure-seeking and Conviction-based happiness.

Let's begin by illustrating the differences between pleasure-seeking happiness and conviction-based happiness by using a radical figure like Malcolm X. The childhood dream of Malcolm X was to become a great attorney; that dream was spoiled by hatred and racial discrimination. In frustration and disappointment, he pursued a lifestyle of pleasure by partying, taking drugs, and sexual licentiousness. By the time he was 21, he was addicted to cocaine and found himself in jail for burglary.

At this point, it's safe to say he has experienced a lot of pleasure; however, his lifestyle was inconsistent and showed that he was still miserable. He then embraced the teachings of the Nation of Islam and began to formulate personal convictions. By channeling his pleasure and confidence as a leader, he found perspective. By leading his followers to rise above social injustice, he found happiness.

Since the days of ancient Greece and Rome, pleasure-seeking socialites have existed. The Greek philosopher Socrates pondered that pleasure was based on human morality, and he suggested that human pleasure resulted from moral good and that pain was of evil.

While another Greek philosopher, Epicurus, believed the greatest destroyer of human happiness was anxiety about the future, especially the fear of the gods and fear of death. The ancient Greeks and Romans popularized these ideas for more than 700 years.

Yet today, the recent sexual revolution of the 1960s was popularized by Playboy magazine's founder Hugh Hefner.

Why should we say that happiness is a human condition so innately a part of our existence that it has become the American fabric of our lives? Thomas Jefferson ascribed and penned unalienable rights endowed by our Creator within the Declaration of Independence as our life, liberty, and the pursuit of happiness.

Some time ago, our Senior Pastor, Dr. Joe Coffey, preached an excellent series of messages about Christ being the center of our lives as Christians.

The sequence in its entirety had a common thread surrounding the use and definition of one Greek word; the Greek word epithymía, which translates into English as desire. The word desire conveys a gamma of human longings and emotions. It describes natural cravings like hunger, sex, and even our desire for God. It also describes unnatural desires such as greed and lust. There are a few occasions where desires are ascribed to God himself.

The series illustrated how human desires are like a wheel, and all the spokes must align to the center for there to be a balance. When our desires are out of control, then we are without balance. Listen to how the book of James says it in James 4:1-3: What causes fights and quarrels among you?

Don't they come from your desires that battle within you? You desire but do not have, so you kill. You covet but cannot get what you want, so you quarrel and fight. You do not have it because you do not ask God. When you ask, you do not receive because you ask with wrong motives, that you may spend what you get for your pleasures.

In the Old Testament, the word desire shows up in God's conversion to Cain after he changes the order of worship and attempts to offer a bloodless sacrifice. Genesis 4:6 says: Then the Lord asked Cain, why are you angry? Why is your face downcast? Genesis 4:7 – If you do what is right, will you not be accepted? But if you do not do what is right, sin is crouching at your door; it desires to have you, but you must rule over it.

Here in itself is described as desiring to have Cain. God defines sin crouching as a hungry beast prepared to prey upon him, and he instructs Cain to master it.

The question arises how then do we know if a desire is good or bad? The true answer lies in the object or reason for that desire. If the desire is self-centered, it is terrible because sin is determined to have one's way. Good wishes are the opposite, putting the passion for God's will first. When the

Lord is our greatest desire, all other desires find their proper expression.

Several years ago, as a young Missionary to the nation of Indonesia, I met a young woman that would one day become my wife. While my wife and her family were raised Christian, their grandfathers were of Chinese descent and would define happiness differently. It was enough for me to struggle with the daily concepts between Eastern and Western cultures, but now I had to understand how Chinese people displayed happiness to future generations.

The Chinese mindset is taught that happiness has five essential elements: longevity, wealth, health, virtue, and family (or community). You can see it illustrated best in the statues of the Zen monk called "Happy Buddha." See if you can follow. Oversized ears depict longevity; in Asian cultures, big ears live long. Wealth is shown by the material elements or display of precious metals or gems.

The adoring of gold, silver, jade and precious gemstones worn in the east depicts personal or family wealth. In fact, on a side note, if you were mugged in an Asian country and your gold was considered fake, you would undoubtedly be harmed. Health in most eastern countries is reflected by signs of obesity, as the healthy and well-off have plenty to eat. Virtue is shown in the position of a teacher or holy man of prayer and community in the openness of its display.

In 2009 the tenth anniversary of His Holiness, The Dalai Lama's book (with questions posed by psychiatrist Howard Cutler M.D.) The Art of Happiness; A Handbook for Living was reprinted by Riverhead Books. Maybe you're asking yourself, "Who is the Dalai Lama anyway?" "Well, His Holiness the Fourteenth." "Dalai Lama, Tenzin" Gyatso, is the spiritual and temporal leader of the Tibetan people. He was born in a small village called Taktser in northeastern Tibet.

Born to a peasant family, His Holiness was recognized at the age of two, under Tibetan tradition, as the reincarnation of his predecessor, the 13th Dalai Lama. The Dalai Lamas are the manifestations of the Bodhisattva of Compassion, who chose to reincarnate to serve the people. Dalai Lama means Ocean of Wisdom. Tibetans typically refer to His Holiness as Yeshe Norbu, the Wish-fulfilling Gem, or Kundun, meaning The Presence.

In 1959, he was forced into exile in India after the Chinese military occupation of Tibet. Since 1960 he has resided in

Dharamsala, aptly known as "Little Lhasa," the seat of the Tibetan Government-in-Exile. In 1989 he won the Nobel Prize for Peace and authored several books, including the International Best-Selling book, The Art of Happiness; A Handbook for Living.

In chapter four of this book, he addresses the topic: Reclaiming our Innate State of Happiness, and in the preface of the book, he writes this:

The concept of happiness as an achievable goal, something we can deliberately cultivate through practice and effort, is fundamental to the Buddhist view of happiness. The idea of training the mind has been the cornerstone of Buddhist practice for millennia. So having defined the understanding of happiness from several angles, we can now address the question, "What makes us happy?"

Bibliography

Pope Francis announced she would be canonized as a Saint.

Roy Exum: Saint Teresa's Authority - Chattanoogan.com. https://www.chattanoogan.com/2015/12/19/314649/Roy-Exum-Saint-Teresas-Authority.aspx

For I was hungry, and you gave me food, I was thirsty, and you gave me drink, I was a stranger, and you made me welcome, lacking clothes and you clothed me, sick and you visited me, in prison and you came to see me.

Society of St. Vincent De Paul.

http://www.stfrancistownsend.org/councilscommittees-2/society-of-st-vincent-de-paul/

People are often unreasonable and self-centered. Forgive them anyway. If you are kind, people may accuse you of ulterior motives. Be kind anyway. If you are honest, people may cheat you. Be honest anyway. If you find happiness, people may be jealous. Be happy anyway. The good you do today may be forgotten tomorrow. Do well anyway

"Morrin Community Calendar Darcy Graham." The

Drumheller Mail, Alberta Weekly Newspaper Association, 24 Sept. 2014, p. A.12.

It was never between you and them anyway.

— Mother Teresa

Mother Teresa Quote: "The good you do today may be ....
https://quotefancy.com/quote/868720/Mother-Teresa-The-good-you-do-today-may-be-forgotten-tomorrow-Do-good-anyway-Give-the

In The Garden

I come to the garden alone,

In the Garden > Lyrics | Charles A. Miles - Timeless Truths.

https://library.timelesstruths.org/music/In_the_Garden/

The Art of Happiness; A Handbook for Living

Rao, Krishna, et al. "Antiaging Effects of an Intensive Mind and Body Therapeutic Program through Enhancement of Telomerase Activity and Adult Stem Cell Counts." Journal of Stem Cells, vol. 10, no. 2, Nova Science Publishers, Inc., Apr. 2015, p. 107.

Dalai Lama, Tenzin Gyatso, is the spiritual and temporal leader of the Tibetan people. He was born in a small village called Taktser in northeastern Tibet. Born to a peasant family, His Holiness was recognized at the age of two

The 14th Dalai Lama – Biographical - NobelPrize.org. https://www.nobelprize.org/prizes/peace/1989/lama/biographical/

The concept of happiness as an achievable goal, something we can deliberately cultivate through practice and effort, is fundamental to the Buddhist view of happiness. The idea of training the mind has been the cornerstone of Buddhist practice for millennia.

Positive psychology | Healthymemory's Blog. https://healthymemory.wordpress.com/tag/positive-psychology/

RUNNING HEAD: Concepts of Happiness

Concepts of Happiness Across Time and Cultures

Shigehiro Oishi, University of Virginia

Jesse Graham, University of Southern California

Selin Kesebir, London Business School

Iolanda Costa Galinha, Universidade Autónoma de Lisboa

In press, Personality and Social Psychology Bulletin

The Legatum

Prosperity IndexTM2019

A tool for transformation

I think it's safe to say that happiness is not determined so much by objective factors but by how you feel about them.

Satisfaction vs. Happiness – VS Pages.

https://vspages.com/satisfaction-vs-happiness-1141/

in our image, in our likeness, so that they may rule over the fish in the sea, the birds in the sky, the livestock and all the wild animals, and the creatures that move along the ground.

The Biblical Hebrew Word of 'Laabod' Or 'Cultivate' | God TV.

https://godtv.com/laabod-cultivate-biblical-hebrew/

"So God created mankind in his image, in the image of God

he created them; male and female he created them."

Hines-Brigger, Susan. "Caring for Creation." St. Anthony Messenger, vol. 124, no. 5, Franciscan Media, LLC, Oct. 2016, p. 54.

Good and evil. "Since there is no God to will what is good, we must will our good. And since there is no eternal value, we must will the eternal recurrence of the same state of affairs." (Friedrich Nietzsche, 1844-1900)

Apologetics: Is truth objective or subjective?

https://www.truthnet.org/Christianity/Apologetics/Truth2/

The stronger must dominate and not mate with the weaker, which would signify the sacrifice of its own higher nature. Only the born weakling can look upon this principle as cruel, and if he does so, it is merely because he is of a feebler

Volume 1, Chapter 11: Race and People – Christogenea.

https://mk.christogenea.org/references/mein-kampf-book-1-chapter-11

For example, if my boss gives me a deadline for completing a project and a measure to follow,

What's a green nudge? – The ... – The Behaviouralist.

https://thebehaviouralist.com/whats-a-green-nudge/

I had a close friend in high school that was quite comical, and occasionally he would grab me by the arm and drag me several feet while muttering

Prophets, Apostles, and Mental Illness – WHAT REALLY HAPPENED.

https://www.whatreallyhappened.com/WRHARTICLES/prophets.php

given me, I say to every one of you: Do not think of yourself more highly than you ought, but rather think of yourself with sober judgment, in accordance with the faith God has distributed to each of you."

Hill, Peter, et al. "Glad Intellectual Dependence on God: A Theistic Account of Intellectual Humility." Journal of Psychology and Christianity, vol. 37, no. 3, Christian Association for Psychological Studies, Inc., Oct. 2018, p. 195.

The human visual system is complex and amazingly adaptive. It can change focus to see objects both near and far,

Overworked Eyes: Will Your Computer Make You Go Blind

https://www.huffpost.com/entry/eye-strain_b_1591414

Jesus in Numbers – Discover Historic Jesus.
https://discoverhistoricjesus.com/jesus-in-numbers/

Jesus in Numbers – Discover Historic Jesus.

https://discoverhistoricjesus.com/jesus-in-numbers/

"My Utmost for His Highest, " a dear Scottish brother in Christ." Within this book, he makes a statement that brings repentance into focus: "If you ever cease to understand the value of repentance, you allow yourself to remain in sin."

Repentance – My Utmost for His Highest.

https://utmost.org/repentance/

The World's Happiest (And Saddest) Countries.
https://www.forbes.com/sites/christopherhelman/2011/12/0
7/the-worlds-happiest-and-saddest-countries/

The World's Happiest (And Saddest) Countries.

https://www.forbes.com/sites/christopherhelman/2011/12/0

7/the-worlds-happiest-and-saddest-countries/

Having more money might actually make people happier, according to a study of people's income levels and their reported levels of happiness. People with higher incomes reported feeling more satisfied with their lives overall. For instance, 35% of respondents who reported making $35,000 US Dollars (USD) or less each year said they felt very happy,

Can Money Buy Happiness?

https://www.wise-geek.com/can-money-buy-happiness.htm

Smiling has been found to increase feelings of happiness. Psychologists believe this is because the brain interprets the flexing of specific muscles

Can Smiling Make You Happier? – wiseGEEK.

https://www.wise-geek.com/can-smiling-make-you-happier.htm

Chapter Six

Tuscany Italy

What Makes Us Happy?

There are certain fundamental things in life that are more likely to make us feel happy. For example, chances are you'll probably have a generally more optimistic and positive outlook if your basic needs are met through things like financial stability, good health, and a sense of fulfillment and purpose in daily life.

But I ask, is it that simple? Happiness can be determined by a lot of things that we cannot explain. There are millionaires and billionaires who have all the resources and money in the world. They, even from an outside perspective, have stable family lives, and yet they are stricken with depression. Many of them have even committed suicide. So, things might not be as straightforward as they seem. What many of these people have in common is their lack of belief in a higher power, the divine.

Now, this might sound preachy, but it is confirmed when you have achieved and enjoyed everything life has to offer, you tend to contemplate, and usually, the question that keeps entering the dark matter of our brains is, "What is next?"

This question will always be at the forefront of our lives. The only guarantee in life is death, and this fact is something none of us can run away from. We can ignore it for as long as possible, but it's a fact of life. Death is part and parcel of life. A great philosopher once said death created time so that it can grow the things it kills. Knowing that life is short is one thing but experiencing your life till old age is an entirely different matter. Hence the question of what makes us happy holds a more significant meaning.

One day a co-worker said to me, "Russ, you have got to be one of the happiest people I have ever met. What makes you so happy all of the time?" It was probably a rhetorical question, but my answer was relatively short and straightforward. "It's because of what Jesus Christ has done in my life." I honestly can't remember the last time I felt unhappy for longer than 20 minutes, and it's because I have learned the meaning of one significant Bible verse.

1 Peter 5:7 says, "Cast all your anxiety on him because he cares for you."

You see, that word cast makes all the difference in understanding what the text is trying to convey. Looking at that word in the original Greek language gives us a picture of throwing a javelin with great force. It is translated as "epiripto," which is two words, "epi" and "ripto."(Strong's Exhaustive Concordance, 1977, 1909 and 4496) The word "epi" means upon, as on top of something. The word "ripto" means to hurl, throw, or cast, and it often points to throwing violently or flinging something with great force.

God has not designed us to carry the burden of worry and anxiety, and this load is too much for the human mind and body to bear. Medical science suggests that the central nervous system cannot tolerate stress for extended periods. While we may manage it for short periods, the physical body and mind will eventually break down under pressure. The primary source of sickness in the Western Hemisphere is our daily stress levels. People are not fashioned to carry the anxieties and worries of this life alone.

Taking care of your physical health is important, but the mind is of great importance as well because the stronger the mind, the better your body's chances of fighting off diseases and illness. God has made us strong and resilient, but continuous stress will lead to our downfall and complete breakdown of our body and soul. In these times, it is important to remember that our life is short and needs to be lived in a certain way.

The last portion of 1 Peter 5:7 reads, "...because he cares for you." You have to genuinely know that someone cares for you before you begin to unload your cares upon them.

This means anything that causes you worry or anxiety is thrown far from you regardless of the source. Throw it far and fast as if you were throwing a spear. Peter says cast it over the shoulders of Jesus Christ because "He careth for you." The word "careth" is taken from the Greek word "Melo," which is defined in this way as "to be an object of care" or to give painful and meticulous attention. (Strong's Exhaustive Concordance, 3199)

Peter uses this word to assure us that Jesus does care about us, and he is deeply concerned about the things weighing heavily on our hearts. Jesus gives meticulous attention to the details concerning us, and he is interested in every facet of our lives. The saddest part of this is that not everyone is convinced that they are loveable and that someone could care that much for them. On the other hand, some people enjoy keeping themselves busy with worry and anxiety. My grandmother used to say worry is like a rocking chair; it keeps you busy but doesn't get you anywhere.

We all want to be happy because, after all, happiness is

helpful for many things. Think about it for a moment. Happiness improves our physical and mental health, and it enhances our creativity. It even enables us to make better decisions as it's harder to be rational when you're unhappy.

Recently, as I reflected on the suicide death of comedian Robin Williams, it reminded me of another talented individual whose story was written in a book entitled "Memoirs of Joseph Grimaldi." (Grimaldi 1838) In London during the nineteenth century, often in the Covent Garden Theatre, a talented pantomime acted out Harlequin and Mother Goose. His performances were said to be an antidote for the melodically, as the crowds jeered with laughter as tears streamed down their faces. Joseph Grimaldi (1778-1837) was indeed one of England's most famous clowns, but his personal life was anything but happy as he suffered from alcoholism and bouts of deep depression. Solomon reminds us in Proverbs 14:13, "Even in laughter the heart may ache, and rejoicing may end in grief."

There is an over-abundance of research on factors that correlate with the individuals' assessments of their happiness and the things that genuinely bring satisfaction.

So then, what factors are there that we can eliminate and

clearly say these factors don't correlate with happiness? My list might differ from yours and does not mean to be a clinical study. I have included six things that appear to be least likely to affect changes in personal happiness: intelligence, age, gender, physical attractiveness, parenthood, and money (above the poverty line). On the other hand, the factors that slightly affect our state of happiness, in my opinion (unless excessive), are health, social activity, and culture (in terms of how well you think you fit into your environment).

There are so many clarifiers needed for this topic it's almost a personal evaluation. The aptest factors to correlate with our sense of personal happiness are religiosity (formulating personal change), family DNA, and a sense of fulfillment in our work. The most pivoting question remains, is correlation enough? We need to know what causes happiness in our lives and what triggers unhappiness.

Most importantly, what do we do with those bothersome feelings that tell us that we are just not happy? I think it's safe to say that happiness is not determined so much by objective factors but by how you feel about them. So, can we say that happiness is both subjective and relative simultaneously?

We would have to re-visit our previous questions centered around the absolute truth to answer this question. Are you ready? From the very beginning of time, man has been given a choice to make life decisions based on right and wrong. This concept of truth focuses on one major event- the creation of man in Genesis 1:26-27 (according to those of the Judo-Christian belief system). In verse 26 it reads:

Then God said, "Let us make humanity in our image, in our likeness, so that they may rule over the fish in the sea and the birds in the sky, over the livestock and all the wild animals, and overall, the creatures that move along the ground."

Then in verse 27, it continues: "So God created mankind in his image, in the image of God he created them; male and female he created them." Without boring you, and to give these two verses the proper textual interpretation they deserve, we have to entertain the central question of what is being said in the first two words- "Let us." First of all, the focus is on God at this point, and by the context, we hear it saying, "Let us."

To English-speaking individuals, it implies that we are talking about more than one God. Surprisingly enough, the

Hebrew language also means a plural use of the word "god" in its translation "Elohim" (or "Eloah"). This is the beginning argument for the Christian view of God as one but in three persons (Father, Son, and Holy Spirit.) What then keeps this verse from saying, "gods created mankind?" (Strong's Exhaustive Concordance, 430, 433) While I know it's not good practice to answer a question with another question, let me pose a hypothetic question for the sake of confusion. Does the Hebrew word for God ("Elohim") always means "gods" since it is structurally plural? The answer to that question is- it does not.

The grammar structure tells us if it is singular or plural by rule.

While there are times when the meaning is entirely ambiguous (not having any grammatical-contextual clues), this does not appear to be the case in Genesis 1. So, generally speaking, there are verses in the Old Testament that speak of plural gods (Gen 35:7; Gen 22:3; Gen 20:6 and Psa 82:1).

However, for the sake of being called a "heretic," it is my opinion that God in its plural sense is referring to members of God's counsel (or the Triune God, Psalm 82 is the best example of that- "God stands in the divine assembly; he judges among the gods.") So having said all of that, the biblical structure of the morality of humanity is being created in the image of the Creator.

When we listened to our dear friend Max Edelman share his story about the Holocaust, we unconsciously judged who was "right" and "wrong." We have to draw from a knowledge base of what makes those actions right or wrong. How does one determine Nazi Germany's "wrongness" in their attempted conquest of the world and killing innocent people?

Do you recall referring to the Nuremberg Laws and the trials following the Second World War?

Those trials sought to make the same determination by asking difficult questions of what basis can we prosecute the Nazis for their actions, and how do we determine what are to be considered crimes against humanity?

This might surprise you, but Germany used the Darwinian principle of survival of the fittest to establish the Nuremberg Laws as the platform for truth. Germany viewed their nation and race as superior to the rest of the world and began dehumanizing those they regarded as weaker or inferior.

This truth was derived from German philosopher Friedrich Wilhelm Nietzsche who went insane at 45 years of age and taught that man is the source of good and evil. "Since there is no God to will what is good, we must will our good. And since there is no eternal value, we must will the eternal recurrence of the same state of affairs." (Friedrich Nietzsche, 1844-1900)

With such a strong influence on German thinking, is it surprising that Adolph Hitler also adopted Nietzsche's view of truth? I believe that a false concept of truth resulted from millions of people dying during The Holocaust. In Adolf Hitler's biography "Mein Kampf" he writes these words:

The stronger must dominate and not mate with the weaker, which would signify the sacrifice of its own higher nature. Only the born weakling can look upon this principle as cruel, and if he does so, it is merely because he is of a feebler mind and narrower mind; for if such a law did not direct the process of evolution, then the higher development of organic life would not be conceivable at all. If nature does not wish that weaker individuals should mate with stronger, she wishes even less that a superior race should intermingle with an inferior one; because in such a case, all her efforts, throughout hundreds of thousands of years, to establish an evolutionary higher stage of being, may thus be rendered futile.

The difficult questions posed by the Nazis during the Nuremberg trials are the same questions confronting us today. We are still formulating questions based on Moral Law and asking if the truth is subjective (what we perceive to be reality) or objective (a part of reality as we know it). Many of my non-Christian friends have told me that the book of John offends them, and more specifically, John 14:6: Jesus answered, "I am the way and the truth and the life. No one comes to the Father except through me."

Jesus was saying for us to settle the question of Moral Law, we must know that He is objective truth, and everything else must be subjective to His Word. So, by definition, absolute truth must remain faithful to all people, at all times and in all places, and relative truth is subject to the holder of truth.

So, for example, if the truth were relative to someone like Billy Graham, who believes God exists, and an Atheist who believes God does not exist, both would have to be correct. God would have to live and not exist. On the other hand, a Christian who believes in the historical fact that Jesus Christ died on the Cross and someone of another religion believes

He did not, then both would be right for relative truth to be absolute.

While I am not a clinical psychologist or even a great philosopher, the Bible shows that the answer to our happiness rests in keeping a balance in our relationships. We must have balance horizontally in our relationship with God and vertical with one another. Many of you are thinking about how difficult it is to balance your relationships in light of the expectations of God's Laws and the high standard of others. I submit to you that happiness does have an element of anticipation, and too often, it is a false expectation.

For those of you who are (or have been) married, you recall the high expectations you had for your mate, and only to discover after a short time that they could not live up to those unreal expectations. I don't believe we should completely erase our expectations because having no standard is quite dangerous. For example, if my boss gives me a deadline for completing a project and a measure to follow, I am expected to do so or find other employment.

However, in relationships, we must allow people the space to be themselves and still change for the best. God has called us to observe part of the horizontal and vertical balance.

So having defined our topic and narrowed our vantage point, let's examine some ways that we can become happier people. We have earlier alluded to the fact that human beings are very complex individuals and that happiness is not a simple one.

Farther more, I must be forthright in saying my credentials dictate our approach. Instead, we will not be taking a clinical approach to this matter but from a social and theological perspective.

Moreover, happiness will be achieved differently at different stages of personal development. For instance, a person suffering from depression due to chemical imbalance may find improvement in medicine instead of learning better social skills.

However, you will not hear me encourage the development of healthy self-esteem within a culture flooded with solutions of self-help and aggravated assessments of personal inferiority. I make that statement lightly, having worked and lived in dysfunctional and abusive environments.

If I had a megaphone on top of the tallest building in the most populous city in America, I would say, "Self-improvement

159

is not taking you in the right direction."

I had a close friend in high school that was quite comical, and occasionally he would grab me by the arm and drag me several feet while muttering the line, "Where are you taking me." That is my perspective on the self-improvement industry. While disguised as a friend, it will always take us down a path we never intended.

In Romans 12:3, the Apostle Paul says: "For by the grace was given me I say to every one of you: Do not think of yourself more highly than you ought, but rather think of yourself with sober judgment, in accordance with the faith God has distributed to each of you."

The problem, as I see it, is not personal inferiority but our spiritual blindness.

In 2 Peter 1:3-9, the Apostle Peter is speaking to a group of Christians about what I will call "life instructions" and concludes verse nine by saying: "But whoever does not have them is nearsighted and blind, forgetting that they have been cleansed from their past sins." (In an older translation, it says they are blind and cannot see afar off.)

That statement has always intrigued me because of my

background in the optical field. It's as if Peter is saying, "Hey, if you don't get this, then you need some spiritual eyeglasses to see where God has brought you."

In an article by Dr. Robert Joyce, O.D. entitled "Overworked Eyes: Will Your Computer Make You Go Blind?" human eyesight is explained in this fashion:

The human visual system is complex and amazingly adaptive. It can change focus to see objects both near and far, and it can change to see under bright or dark conditions. With the help of 140 million neurons in the visual cortex, it can identify, classify, analyze and react to approximately 12 to 15 one-million-point images per second.

Dr. Jeffrey Anshel, O.D. (author of "Visual Ergonomics in the Workplace") states: "Your eyes are happiest when used for a variety of tasks utilizing a variety of focal distances with a variety of properly aligned light sources."

On the other hand, "spiritual myopia" is when we have lost our perspective of eternal value but continue to grip things of temporal worth. For a Christian, it is the focus of "lordship." Jesus Christ may have saved your eternal soul, but He has yet to become the Lord of your life. As children, we used to tell our siblings, "You're not the boss of me," but

161

now, as mature Christians, we must know that Jesus is the boss of every area of our life.

That is what lordship means, and until our desires become His, we are still in control. Also, when we attempt to engage in any of the suggested methods for becoming happier people, we must first ask ourselves: "does the starting point require some mastery over procrastination?" Without such a question, we may find ourselves in an unending cycle of "yesterday."

Let me begin by suggesting that if you suffer from a severe illness, such as clinical depression, anxiety, paranoia, schizophrenia, or others, you must seek professional help. Otherwise, you will quickly find yourself in a self-destructive pattern that will drain you of all your natural resources.

My first attempt to become happier would begin with a short season of introspection or self-examination and soul-searching. From a biblical perspective, we see that we were born in sin apart from God and need a savior. We are not getting better on our own but are in a spiral of decay.

I mentioned that this should be a "short season of introspection" because an answer is imperative once you realize just how needy you are. This is not a place you should remain, for hope does not abide there.

Only when you have reached the plateau of discovery that I am a sinner lost and separate from Creator God and in need of a savor can I exit the door and expect success in another. At that point, we have learned that Jesus Christ is both the answer and the question all rolled into one. The book of Romans conveys it this way: (Romans 10: 8-10) "The word is near you; it is in your mouth and your heart..." (The gospel message we are proclaiming concerning faith in Jesus Christ).

If you declare with your mouth, "Jesus is Lord," and believe in your heart that God raised him from the dead, you will be saved. For it is with your heart that you think and are justified, and it is with your mouth that you profess your faith and are saved.

As you can see, a "short season of introspection" should process into a period of repentance. Repentance is when we become remorse or contrite in our heart, realizing our eternal destiny leaves us lost, and without God, we completely stop and turn around. The prophet Isaiah said it this way in Isaiah 55:6-7:

Seek the Lord while he may be found; call on him nearby. Let the wicked forsake his way and the evil man his thoughts. Let him turn to the Lord, and he will have mercy on him, and to our God, for he will freely pardon.

After repentance, God enables changes as the Holy Spirit comes to live inside you. Religion tells us we have to get our act together and then come to God to be changed, but relationship tells us to go as we are, and God will live inside of us to become the source of change. The book of Romans says it this way in Romans 12:1-2:

Therefore, I urge you, brothers, in view of God's mercy, to offer your bodies as living sacrifices, holy and pleasing to God; this is your spiritual act of worship. Do not conform any longer to the pattern of this world, but be transformed by the renewing of your mind. Then you will be able to test and approve what God's will is, his good, pleasing, and perfect will.

There is a controversy over the question of why we do good work. Is it to please God or as a by-product of what God has already done in the person and works of Jesus Christ? James, the earthly brother of Jesus, answers this question for us in James1:25:

But the man who looks into the perfect mirror of God's law, the law of liberty (or freedom), and makes a habit of so doing is not the man who sees and forgets. He puts that law into practice, and he wins true happiness. (J. B. Phillips. "The New Testament in Modern English" 1962 HarperCollins)

Repentance is taking in God's point of view and considering things from His perspective and not our own.

In Proverbs 14:12, King Solomon says it like this: "There is a way that seems right to a man, but in the end, it leads to death." Let me illustrate this point with an Old Testament story that depicts the Hebrews following Moses in the wilderness when all of a sudden, the entire camp was bitten by poisonous snakes. In the book of Numbers 21:8-9, it reads:

The Lord said to Moses, "Make a snake and put it up on a pole; anyone who is bitten can look at it and live." So, Moses made a bronze snake and put it up on a pole. Then when anyone was bitten by a snake and looked at the bronze snake, they lived.

Let's imagine that we are in this very situation as poisonous snakes have bitten everyone around us, and while we are not yet dead, the prospect looks very likely.

Suddenly a loud voice bellows throughout the camp as someone suggests: "We must do something. We must save ourselves!" But how do we? Various ideas surface but are unlearned; we know nothing about how the poison circulates throughout the human body. Just then, someone suggests, "If you run around frantically, maybe it will work out the poison!" A few people try this and die in the process.

Others may try to convince themselves that they have not been bitten or that the snakes were not poisonous and form little groups to delude each other while dying and get even worse. Then we hear the trusted voice of Moses saying, 'If you look at the bronze snake that has been lifted on this pole, you will live. If you do not, no matter what else you do, you will surely die.' I can't help thinking that people found this solution far too simple and wanted to do something on their own instead.

The question remains today, "do you believe in God's solution?" In John 3:14, Jesus brings the Old Testament event into perspective by making the parallel between the crucifixions: "Just as Moses lifted the snake in the desert, so the Son of Man must be lifted." Oswald Chambers (1874 - 1917) wrote a classic devotional entitled: "My Utmost for His Highest, "a dear Scottish brother in Christ." Within this book, he makes a statement that brings repentance into focus: "If you ever cease to understand the value of repentance, you allow yourself to remain in sin."

Once this issue of sin is taken care of, and we realize that God in Christ has nailed it to a cross, then we can do as the writer of Hebrews says in Hebrews 4:16.

Let us then approach God's throne of grace with confidence so that we may receive mercy and find grace to help us in our time of need.

Our confidence comes in the finished works of Jesus Christ and His righteousness alone.

Paul then admonishes us in Romans 13: 11-14 to live godly lives as though today was our last day upon this earth:

And do this, understanding the present time: The hour had already come for you to wake up from your slumber because our salvation is nearer now than when we first believed. The night is nearly over; the day is almost here.

So let us put aside the deeds of darkness and put on the armor of light. Let us behave decently, as in the daytime, not in carousing and drunkenness, not in sexual immorality and debauchery, not in dissension and jealousy. Rather, clothe yourselves with the Lord Jesus Christ, and do not think about how to gratify the desires of the flesh. Whatever happiness is to you and by whatever standard you choose to follow, it's clear that some conditions cause it to blossom in due season.

By way of measurement, The Legatum Prosperity Index (part of billionaire Christopher Chandler's Dubai-based Legatum Group) is an assessment of global wealth and overall wellbeing that focuses on 142 countries around the world in eight distinct categories: Economy; Education; Entrepreneurship & Opportunity; Governance; Health; Personal Freedom; Safety & Security; and Social Capital. This index examines the 142 nations (using the eight categories) to view 96% of the world's factors. Thereby helping us determine what things make us happy. For 2013 statics:

Most people would agree that our quality of life is more critical in determining our happiness and prosperity than our country's GDP.

That makes me wonder why some nations are happier and more satisfied than others. Let us consider the indexes example of countries like Ghana and South Korea as examples, as both had similar GDPs in the 1950s but now have gone in such different directions as in 2022, Korea's $ 28075 per capita and Ghana's just $ 910.00.

By this standard which country would be considered the happiest in the world? In 2022 Switzerland topped the overall quality of life list. To obtain this rating, a country must score highly in all eight categories.

The highest taxes in Switzerland levied at the communal level can be found in Chancy and Avully and is 51 percent of basic cantonal tax.

Democracies appeared to be much happier, as they felt they had some input into how their countries were run. These same countries also have great civil liberties.

On the other hand, the Aussies have abolished trade protections, freed labor markets, reformed strict immigration laws, and become one of the world's most flexible economies. At the same time, the U.S. stands out with a fifth-place rank in entrepreneurism and first place in health, thanks to the world's highest level of health spending, significant vaccination levels, clean water, plentiful food, and beautiful natural scenery.

So, by way of contrast, who was considered the "saddest

country in the world?" The Central African Republic was considered the worst by the 2022 index. The Central African Republic is also estimated to be the unhealthiest country as well as the worst country in which to be young.

On the note of entrepreneurs in America, I often hear, 'can it (money) buy happiness? I subscribe to a website that emails tidbits of information, and I received a segment that caught my eye entitled "Can Money Buy Happiness" The piece reads:

Having more money might actually make people happier, according to a study of people's income levels and their reported levels of happiness. People with higher incomes reported feeling more satisfied with their lives overall. For instance, 35% of respondents who reported making $35,000 US Dollars (USD) or less each year said they felt very happy, while all respondents who were making more than USD 500,000 reported the same.

Previously, one of the widely accepted theories about money and happiness was the Easterlin paradox, a 1974 theory by economist Richard Easterlin, which stated that an average increase in income did not directly result in a moderate rise in happiness. Then it went on to add three more fascinating pieces of information:

Americans earning more than $85,000 a year are happier than those who earn less. A study in Proceedings of the National Academy of Sciences found that the more you earn, the happier you are. Previous research found that happiness plateaued when earning $75,000 a year

One study that gave participants money to spend either on themselves or others found that those who consumed the money on other people reported feeling happier than those who spent it on themselves.

A 2022 study found that Switzerland was the happiest country globally, and its average net income was the second-highest in the world.

In light of all the data we just read about happiness and physically expressing emotions, the simple act of smiling can trigger happiness in the human brain.

Smiling has been found to increase feelings of happiness. Psychologists believe this is because the brain interprets the flexing of specific muscles to indicate a particular mood. For example, the zygomatic major is the facial muscle responsible for controlling the corners of the mouth. When

171

this muscle is flexed, it is thought to trigger the neurological response that controls emotion. Another possibility is that smiling while around other people lead them to smile back, and the brain reads this as a social cue to feel happy.

Bibliography

http://www.prosperity.com/#!/ranking

https://www.nicerx.com/happy-nations/

Currently updated statics for The Legatum Prosperity Index can be found at their website https://www.prosperity.com/.

07/05/2012, The Huffington Post. Website:

http://www.huffingtonpost.com/robert-joyce-od/eye-strain_b_1591414.html

(Refer to site: http://www.wisegeek.com/can-smiling-make-you-happier.htm)

Who would guess you could trick your brain into thinking you were happy by just smiling?

Chapter Seven

<u>John Brown's Blessing</u>

Happy Capitalism

In this chapter, I would like to look at a culture that is quite mysterious to many in the western hemisphere and, strangely enough, in the eastern. This culture is Japan, and our focus will be on their quest for happiness following World War II.

But before that, we have to look at Capitalism. Capitalism is essentially an economic system in which private actors own and control property in accordance with their interests, and demand and supply freely set prices in markets in a way that can serve the best interests of society.

The primary feature of capitalism is the motive to make a profit. Capitalism has been around for quite some time and is a well-known economic system around the world. It has been fruitful for the rich especially, but the ones at the lower end have suffered because it is a system that encourages you to make the most amount of wealth at the cost of paying others less, and it has a very stringed trickle-down effect which does not bode well for the majority.

The United States is known as the richest country in the world, and henceforth, this system works well enough in their country, but those who are unemployed usually don't get the benefits of what the system has to offer. Those people don't even have the option of hospitals as their employment are directly connected to Medicare, not to mention medical bills in America are the most expensive in the world because, again, their system is unregulated for the most part because of capitalism. America again is a first-world country so let's take a third-world country example that has a capitalist system. In the sub-continent, there is a country named Pakistan which is a third-world nation.

Pakistan is a third-world country that runs on the Capitalist system, but it is the worst version of it because there is greater corruption as most third-world nations are affected by corruption the most. The poverty line is greater, and opportunities to make money are there, but the minimum wage is far too low to ever escape any economic strife.

Anyway, moving forward, we will now take a closer look at another side of capitalism.

Japan is a fortunate nation in many ways, but the assessment of its declining mortality and growing life expectancy rate leads us to many unanswered questions. Questions like, how amazing are it those Japanese infants do not die during the first precarious months after birth? This situation alone translates into the lowest infant mortality rate on the planet. Japanese people also do not die on the battlefield because their constitution prevents them from going to war.

Furthermore, the limitations to street crimes are off-site by the Asian culture, established by a "community mindset" that creates boundaries and social bonds within neighborhood relations.

Unlike other modern societies, violence within the Japanese culture is hardly known and thereby not a major contributing factor to the cause of death within their community. Fatal traffic accidents are also a missing factor in determining mortality rates as they have been on a steady decline.

So, what then is the leading cause of death in Japan? Medical research shows that coronary heart disease and cancer are the two leading causes of death in Japan, like other modern industrial nations. As a result, unprecedented life expectancy gains in Japan have been experienced (Yanagishita, Guralnik 1988).

At the beginning of the twentieth century, life expectancy rates for males at 44.0 years and 44.8 years for females, which was far below levels in Western countries. However, towards the end of the century, the Japanese topped the list for life expectancy with a massive average of 81.25 years. In 2006 studies showed women living up to 85.6 years, while men at 78.5 years.

Could this evidence be irrefutable to a highly prosperous society that reflects a massive gain in its life expectancy? It is indeed, and we must conclude that longevity has traditionally been regarded as an indication of happiness. That should lead us to believe that Japan would be one of the happiest countries in the modern world.

Japan was showing itself to be more prosperous than ever before. From 1955 to 2005, the GDP per capita grew by 30 percent, and between 1980 and 2000, the Gross National Income (per person) doubled from 2,063,000 yen to 4,084,000 yen.

The Japanese people enjoyed a much higher material wealth than their parents, grandparents, or even previous generations before them. They had much larger homes equipped with state-of-the-art amenities and a more significant spendable income.

Politically, Japan has been living in an environment free from social coercion and, by in large, very peaceful and stable for several generations. They have also enjoyed phenomenal progress in education.

They reflected high school enrollment rates at an increase of more than 30 percent from 1955 to 1970 and approaching the 100 percent mark by the close of the century. Enrollment rates at the university level were at 12.8 percent in 1965 and grew to 41.3 percent in 2003. Also, on a side note, information technicalities are more accessible than ever before.

In the United Nations Human Development Index, Japan has consistently rated among the top ten countries since the 1980s in all three categories of health, education, and overall standard of living.

This shows Japan has been a prosperous, highly educated, healthy, and peaceful population during the first decade of the twenty-first century.

If success is measured by population growth or national and human development, Japan has written a book on success. They are a deliberate and hardworking society, with an industrial policy orchestrated exceptionally well by the Japanese government. They have a strong economy, a high educational achievement standard, and an excellent social healthcare system. These things contribute to Japan's high standard of economic growth and social well-being as a nation.

The question remains does success make people happy, and in what way can we apply the concept of happiness to nations? Can we measure happiness aside from social and economic circumstances? What is the role of culture in the experience, perception, and evaluation of happiness?

This is the reason for our focus on Japan. They are one of the oldest countries on the planet and yet the first non-western country to experience the transition from high mortality and high fertility to low mortality and low fertility in demographics.

In years past, most Asian cultures have lacked the emphasis on personal happiness compared to European cultures. However, the quest for happiness in Japan seems to be widespread. There appears to be a scientific interest in societies showing an increase in wealth and the effects of happiness (Diener and Oishi 2000). Economists have long been of interest in how wealth and happiness are related.

Commonly agreed upon is the correlation between poverty and unhappiness and wealth and happiness. As Epicurus taught, happiness is conceptualized as a good that one must strive to obtain—rather than freedom of pain (aponía) or peace of mind (ataraxía).

Based on this information, the question arises, how would one define greed in a capitalist society, and where would you find balance? Is it not the ideology of capitalism for individuals to focus on the pursuit of happiness and the gain of material possessions; rather than the attitude of contentment? Doesn't capitalism imply that happiness is a by-product of producing and consuming goods that make us richer, wiser, healthier, and more beautiful than the rest?

As a former Missionary married to a woman of Chinese-Indonesian decent, I quickly learned that some things get lost in the translation. How then should the Japanese translate the meaning of the word happiness? The Japanese word most commonly used to translate happiness is shiawase, but it is by no means the only translation. Here are some dictionary definitions of the term. The etymological dictionary Nihongo Kaidoku Jiten (Tokyo: Tōyō Shuppan, 2006) gives four meanings for the word shiawase, which are as follows: kōun means good fortune; okotoba means what you say; meguriawase means meet again by chance, and shiuchi means treatment.

Let us critique the concept of Happy Capitalism as an ideology adhered to by the Japanese people momentarily. Throughout Asia, the "Happy Buddha" symbolizes the whole idea of happiness within the community, while in Japan, it is the ideology of "Happy Capitalism" that prevails.

In the 1990s, the Japanese economy took a turn for the worst, bringing about a realization that they could not maintain their previous standard of living. The format copied from the US had historical bases of reflecting a "bull market," but the "bear market" appeared to be missing from the concept.

The economic insecurities of the market increased while the Japanese population reacted with expressions in large numbers of anxiety, clinical depression, and even suicide. With the post, World War II generations, technically advanced relational communication was also new. Men were working longer hours and away from their families for extended periods, and telephones and computers were developing and merging into new forms of two-dimensional communication.

According to a report by Nippon, suicides did see a slight drop as Japanese suicide fell by 0.4% in 2021 from the previous year, but sadly the rate for female suicides rose for the second year running, and to top it all off, it remained high for youth even in 2021.

This was creating problems worldwide but was significantly impacting the Japanese culture. The Japanese youth of the twenty-first century has become socially withdrawn and clinically depressed, triggering one of the highest suicide rates in the industrialized world. While generally more prosperous, more affluent countries reflect a much higher suicide rating than less affluent ones.

As society withdraws and turns inward, the use of two-dimensional communication rises. While we are connected, we cannot communicate face-to-face (three-dimensional) for extended periods. Thus, we have two generations that lack social practices and forms of etiquette—not knowing (or practicing) the simplest expressions of human interaction, such as words of gratitude and sincerity. It's no wonder we have children who cannot distinguish reality from fantasy. We have a growing number of adults who still haven't learned the difference between emotional infatuation and sexual attraction.

Or what to do when you think you have offended another person. Japan's increase in suicide over a fifty-year cycle suggests two grime conclusions. Japan's most striking accomplishments, physical longevity, and material affluence did not guarantee happiness.

The second thing that God wants you to know about life is that happiness must be purposeful to have to meaning. Since happiness is continuant upon circumstances, it is very different from joy and must be viewed in light of eternity.

Bibliography

At the beginning of the twentieth century, life expectancy rates for males at 44.0

Spatial disparities at death. Age-, sex- and disease.... https://journals.openedition.org/eps/7439

However, towards the end of the century, the Japanese topped the list

Protestantism in England - Musée protestant. https://museeprotestant.org/en/notice/protestantism-in-england/

What is the role of culture in the experience, perception, and evaluation

"South Africa : Telecommunications and Postal Services Hosts Cultural Diversity in a Digital Society Conference." MENA Report, Albawaba (London) Ltd., Sept. 2017, p. n/a.

clinically depressed, triggering one of the highest suicide rates in the industrialized world.

Mental Health and Substance Use in U.S. and 10 Other https://www.commonwealthfund.org/publications/issue-briefs/2020/may/mental-health-conditions-substance-use-comparing-us-other-countries

The second thing God wants you to know about life is that happiness must be purposeful to have to mean.

Constant Struggle | Sought Out Generation. https://soughtoutgen.org/articles/constantstruggle

The Statistical Handbook of Japan https://www.stat.go.jp/english/data/handbook/index.html

That word above all earthly powers, no thanks to them, abideth; the Spirit and the gifts are ours, thru him who with us sideth. Let goods and kindred go, this mortal life also; The body they may kill; God's truth abideth still; his kingdom is forever.

MARTIN LUTHER - A MIGHTY FORTRESS IS OUR GOD LYRICS.

https://www.songlyrics.com/martin-luther/a-mighty-fortress-is-our-god-lyrics/

Think about that for a moment in light of whom you are and the people you interact with regularly

You Can Increase Your Intelligence: 5 Ways to Maximize

https://blogs.scientificamerican.com/guest-blog/you-can-increase-your-intelligence-5-ways-to-maximize-your-cognitive-potential/

There are three stages of salvation that create a wonderful package that God has gifted to us in Christ when we receive His finished works. The first is in the past tense, where God in Christ has saved us from the penalty of sin,

Soteriology - The Doctrine of Salvation | Bible.org.

https://bible.org/article/soteriology-doctrine-salvation

Let's look at Matthew's five women in his record and why he does so. Firstly, there is Tamar in Genesis 38:6-30. Tamar was the daughter-in-law of Judah. She was also a childless widow who was given to her brother-in-law after her husband's death. By this marriage, her offspring would continue the name and inheritance of the deceased.

A STUDY OF THE HARMONY OF THE GOSPELS.

http://www.vscoc.org/Workbooks/Harmony_bk1.htm

187

being Mary's husband, Joseph was considered the father of Jesus. Since Jesus was born into Joseph's family, he was a legal heir. Through Joseph, Jesus obtained a rightful claim to the throne of David.

Joseph, son of Jacob: Family tree by Cecelia HOGUE...

https://gw.geneanet.org/chogue?lang=en&n=jacob&oc=1&p=joseph+son+of

instruct certain men not to teach strange doctrines nor to pay attention to myths and endless genealogies, which give rise to mere speculation rather than furthering the administration of God

Luke 1 - The Birth of John the Baptist.

http://ocbubble.com/nautilus/videos/Luke/Luke%201.doc

For some men, straying from these things has turned aside into fruitless discussion.

1 Timothy 1:3-7 - NAS - As I urged you Lit...

https://www.christianity.com/bible/nas/1-timothy/1-3-7

https://www.nippon.com/en/japan-data/h01283/

Chapter Eight

<u>Restoration painting of Michelangelo</u>

Life Inevitable

We've all heard it said that there are two inevitable things in life: death and taxes. Can I suggest a third, from a "geek's" perspective- hard drive crashes? I know that it sounds far too convenient in the age in which we live. Especially when the Obama Administration has had the IRS and the Federal Election Commission lose valuable data stored on hard drives that were never backed up. But tell me you've never had a hard drive crash, and I'm likely you say I don't believe you.

I have been in the IT field for several years, and while computer hardware has changed, practices and mishandling of data remain as haphazard as ever before. So, knowing there must be human intervention in all of these elements, why would we link it to something as abstract as destiny?

"Destiny is what you make it," one man said to me. I find this phrase just as ambiguous as saying, "He was a self-made millionaire." The bottom line is no one lives or dies unto themselves, and like a network, we must all interact with other people. While it is true that you came into this world naked and holding nothing, we will all face the grim reality of death one day.

190

So as the saying goes, "Every soul shall taste death" We are all on a timer, which will run out sooner or later; like most things in life, death is the most inevitable. The only guarantee you will get in life is death itself. It is a thing that all of us will face in one form or another, either through our deaths or the deaths of our loved ones. It is a tough pill to swallow, knowing our time on this earth is limited but then again, if it wasn't, how would we know how meaningful the people in our lives were?

Knowing it will all help put things into perspective, and this is where religion plays a big part. Many people are at peace with death because they know there is a destination beyond this one. This gives us peace because there is nothing worse than knowing that there is nothing beyond this life and that only darkness awaits or, even worse, nothingness.

One atheist I knew had a near-death experience, and when he went under and was almost presumed dead, he told me about what he saw when he was under. After he woke up, he distinctly remembered something dark, but the darkness he saw and felt wasn't one of extreme sadness or coldness. But the darkness he talked about felt warm. He said within that warm darkness, he saw his deceased daughter and also his father, who was also deceased.

It was like everything that he ever loved waiting for him to cross over and all he had to do was let go. Now what he experienced might be explained through different reasoning or explanations, but ultimately, I saw it as something else. I saw it as God's grace which is full of love and mercy. Even if this man didn't believe in Christ, he certainly felt his love. We cannot understand God's wisdom and judgment fully because he is beyond our understanding. Though his love and grace are something inevitable.

Destiny is most generally looked at within the span of one person's lifetime unless they are of royal descent, then their family heritage most often shapes the outcome of who they will become.

Have you ever heard someone say, "Sometimes, life just hands us the inevitable?" That suggests that some things are built into life and can't be explained and that they are somehow a part of the package you were delivered. This is why I believe we need to see destiny in its proper perspective.

Destiny is already written; what will happen has already happened. In scientific terms, this is also called Murphy's Law which Lehman's term means what will happen regardless. Destiny has a lot to do with time and how we perceive it. All of us see time as something linear, but that is the human perspective and experience; God sees time from a 5th-dimensional perspective, meaning he sees time as a flat circle.

I was stunned when I read the book of Revelations and saw the vision that God gave to the Apostle John. God conveys things to John that seem far beyond his comprehension, not to mention the vocabulary needed to express it to his generation.

However, considering John knew both the Greek and Hebrew languages, it seems to be more sufficient. The Hebrew language can express great passion and illustrate visional context, whereas the Greek language articulates words in a legalistic fashion needed to reach the educational and intellectual upper class.

The most astonishing thing about the revelation to John is that it brings us back to the very beginning of time. Back to the garden where things were more straightforward, and intimacy between God and humanity existed in its purest form. A time spoke of by the prophets of old where society would enjoy the fruits of his labor, and nations would beat their weapons into plow shears. Where peace would rule our hearts and minds, and the animal kingdom would be at rest as the lion and lamb would lie down together. This is destiny revealed and unfolds into the perfect plan of Creator God.

Jesus spoke of a time in the gospels of Matthew, Mark, and Luke where God would manifest Himself so that it would appear as though He were ruling and reining before the time became visible. Jesus called it the Kingdom of God (or its equivalent form Kingdom of Heaven). In his gospel,

I especially enjoy the way Matthew draws the critical elements of the teachings of Jesus and the Old Testament to characterize a relationship between God and humanity. A relationship that is so inherent that it evokes the notion of the "Lordship of God." I believe Matthew uses the term Kingdom of Heaven because of his Jewish audience and their restrictions on using the name of God. On the other hand, Paul takes it a step further by pointing out that it's not a matter of keeping a religious code but a lifestyle that flows from the inside out.

In the book of Romans 14:17, Paul says: "For the kingdom of God is not a matter of eating and drinking, but of righteousness, peace and joy in the Holy Spirit."

The Apostle John tells Christians to live life as though Christ's return was imminent within their lifetime. In 1 John 3:2-3, it says: Beloved, now we are children of God, and it has not appeared as yet what we will be. We know that we will be like Him when He seems because we will see Him just as He is. And everyone who has this hope fixed on Him purifies himself, just as He is pure.

Did you catch that? He infers that if you have this hope of Christ's returning, then you will reserve yourself for this truth alone. You won't allow yourself to be entangled with the cares of this life. You won't be derailed by temporary things that bring the war within your members. It will become apparent to all those around you that your life is governed by guidance, not by this world. You will rest in the hope of your destiny and walk as though you were in it.

The Latin word for destiny is *destinare*; it implies that we are somehow capable of determining the beginning from the ending and aspire to do great things. Destiny becomes more than just a human endeavor that we strive to see fulfillment and purpose, but a focal point to which we hope for closure or reward. Many define destiny as our choices in life and how adaptable we are to change (or fate).

195

Parson To Person: Three Things God Wants You To Know About Life

The Apostle Paul illustrates that our destiny in this life is like an athlete who trains with great skill and temperance to focus on the goal alone. They're not interested in second place, but the focal point of their destiny is the prize. 1 Corinthians 9:24-27 reads: Do you not know that those who run in a race all run, but only one receives the prize? Run in such a way that you may win. Everyone who competes in the games exercises self-control in all things. They then do it to receive a perishable wreath, but we can imperishable. Therefore, I run in such a way as not without aim; I box in such a way as not beating the air, but I discipline my body and make it my slave so that, after I have preached to others, I myself will not be disqualified.

The question then arises, what PRIZE is Paul talking about here? Is it salvation? Is it Heaven? Is it Riches in this life? What PRIZE are we contending for in this life? It is your destiny in Christ! The designed plan of God for your life and what He has purposed for you. The Prophet Jeremiah says it best in Jeremiah 29:11, For I know the plans I have for you, declares the LORD, plans to prosper you and not to harm you, plans to give you hope and a future.

In Martin Luther's great hymn, A Mighty Fortress Is Our God (Trans. by Frederick H. Hedge), we are inspired to see things in light of the focused destiny of God's eternal plan. The hymn writer pens, A mighty fortress is our God. That word above all earthly powers, no thanks to them, abideth; the Spirit and the gifts are ours, thru him who with us sideth. Let goods and kindred go, this mortal life also; The body they may kill; God's truth abideth still; his kingdom is forever. What an extraordinary statement of God's plan and destiny working beyond our mortality of just one lifetime!

I have often heard that everyone has a circle of influence of approximately 30,000 people in the average lifetime. Think about that for a moment in light of whom you are and the people you interact with regularly. There's no question in my mind you're influencing people around you, and the real question is, "How are you influencing them?"

In 1 Cor. 13:11-13, it says this: "When I was a child, I used to speak like a child, think like a child, reason like a child; when I became a man, I did away with childish things. For now, we see in a mirror dimly, but then face to face; now I know in part, but then I will know fully just as I also have been fully known. But now faith, hope, love, abide these three; but the greatest of these is love."

How about if we were to paraphrase those verses in this way:

We're squinting in a fog, peering through a mist. But it won't be long before the weather clears and the sun shines bright! We'll see it all then, see it all as clearly as God sees us, knowing him directly just as he knows us! But for right now, until that completeness, we have three things to do to lead us toward that consummation: Trust steadily in God, hope unswervingly, and love extravagantly. And the best of the three is love.

As a missionary to Indonesia, God allowed me to teach in training schools for ministerial students and lecture at a Private (Parochial) University in the capital city of Jakarta on the topic of the 'Principles of Christianity.' During that time, one of my favorite lessons was on the topic of salvation in all of its aspects. In theology, this is known as "soteriology" or the doctrine of salvation. The Bible addresses God's plan to provide a solution to man's problem. In its broadest sense, God seeks to rescue humanity from the power of sin and all that it touches on his life.

God bestows upon humanity the wealth of His grace, in the abundance of life everlasting, and in the power of His glory to become transformed into the likeness of Christ. (Eph. 1:3-8; 2:4-10; 1 Pet. 1:3-5; John 3:16, 36; 10:10).

198

There are three stages of salvation that create a wonderful package that God has gifted to us in Christ when we receive His finished works. The first is in the past tense, where God in Christ has saved us from the penalty of sin, and we are delivered once and for all from sin's penalty and spiritual death. (Luke 7:50; 1 Cor. 1:18; 2 Cor. 2:15; Eph. 2:5, 8; Tit. 3:5; Heb. 7:25; 2 Tim. 1:9).

The second is in the present tense, where God gives us the power to overcome sin in this life. The indwelling power of the Holy Spirit, encompassed with the Bible in the application and with a surrendered nature to the lordship of Christ, brings about a transformed person. (Rom. 6:1-23; 8:2; 2 Cor. 3:18; Gal. 2:19-20; 5:1-26; Phil. 1:19; 2:12-13; 2 Thess. 2:13). The third is in the future tense, where we will receive the ultimate glorification. The power of sin will be diminished completely and forever! To the extent that we will even receive a glorified resurrected body as Jesus had. (Rom. 8:29; 13:11; 1 Pet. 1:5; 1 John 3:2; Phil. 3:12-14).

So then, when we as Christians refer to "being saved," we can see that there is more to that phrase than just the ancient conversation between Jesus and Nicodemus as reviewed in John 3: 6-9 That which is born of the flesh is flesh, and that which is born of the Spirit is a spirit. Do not be amazed that

I said to you that you must be born again. The wind blows where it wishes, and you hear the sound of it but do not know where it comes from and where it is going; so is everyone who is born of the Spirit." Nicodemus said to Him, "How can these things be?

Consequently, we are not just saved in the past tense, but we are being saved, and we will be saved. While it is a finished work that costs us nothing, it costs God everything! When Adam and Eve sinned, it was a conscious effort of their will after God had clearly instructed them otherwise. Following that incident, we don't see it recorded or even implied where God said to the heavens, 'Oh, now look what they have done-they have messed up all my plans for the future!' It didn't catch God by surprise at all because He has given humanity a free will to choose and, in turn, knows what the outcome of our choices will be. So, while the plan of salvation seems to us to have taken a long period after the fall, God was working.

His plan and preparing all the right people in the process. Let's take a closer look at this plan and purpose from the perspective of the Apostles Matthew in chapter 1 of his gospel and Luke in chapter 3 of his account.

The genealogy of Jesus Christ, as told by Matthew, traces the lineage from Abraham to Jesus (which is about 41 generations and is a focus to a Jewish audience). In comparison, Luke records the ancestry from Adam to Jesus (about 76 generations with a Gentile audience). At this point, I have to note that there are quite a few differences and discrepancies existing between the two records. Most startling is that from King David to Jesus, the lineages are entirely different. Matthew's account would trace Jesus' primary (biological) lineage, and Luke's record would follow Jesus' legal lineage.

What is the purpose of these two men in giving two different accounts of the same person- Jesus Christ? Matthew's purpose was to show that Jesus was the promised Messiah sent from God and does a switch in lineage from male to female that many agree would reflect the virgin birth. In contrast, Luke desires to show that Jesus is the Savior of humanity.

Let's look at Matthew's five women in his record and why he does so. Firstly, there is Tamar in Genesis 38:6-30. Tamar was the daughter-in-law of Judah. She was also a childless widow who was given to her brother-in-law after her husband's death. By this marriage, her offspring would continue the name and inheritance of the deceased. This union was later called a Leverite marriage as defined in Deut 25:5-6. Unfortunately, Tamar's brother-in-law refused to have proper intercourse with her. (God killed him for this). Afterward, Judah would not give Tamar to any of his other sons. So, Tamar disguised herself as a harlot and seduced Judah. Through him, she became the mother of Perez.

The second is Rahab, the harlot who lived in Jericho and is known for hiding the spies of Joshua. Because of this, the Israelites spared her life when they conquered Jericho. (Heb 11:30-31) She later became the wife of Salmon and the mother of Boaz.

The third is Ruth, who was not even a Jew by birth but the widow of a Jew and a foreigner from the land of Moab. Her mother-in-law, Naomi, also lived in Moab. Naomi journeyed to Israel after her family died. Her faith was a display to all but especially an example of the "Kinsman Redeemer" that depicted a type of Jesus Christ. While in Israel, Ruth was married to Boaz, one of Naomi's relatives. Ruth later became the mother of Obed, the grandfather of David the King.

The fourth Bathsheba was the wife of Uriah the Hittite, a soldier in King David's army. As you recall from the story, she and David had an adulterous affair. When David discovered Bathsheba was pregnant, he tried to cover it up by summoning Uriah home from war, hoping that Uriah would have intercourse with his wife. Uriah came home to Jerusalem but refused to lay with Bathsheba as long as the armies of Israel were at war. So, David sent Uriah back into battle with orders from which Uriah should be withdrawn when the fighting became fierce. After Uriah was slain in this manner, David took Bathsheba as his wife, and God punished them by killing their first child. Bathsheba later became the mother of Solomon.

The final woman in Matthew's account was Mary, who was the mother of Jesus and the wife of Joseph. She was a virgin when the Holy Spirit conceived Jesus. The record tells us that Joseph was betrothed to Mary when he discovered she was pregnant. He intended to put her away secretly because this was shameful. However, an angel told Joseph what had happened.

So, Joseph took Mary as his wife and kept her a virgin until she gave birth to Jesus. During her pregnancy, Mary spent time with her relative Elizabeth, who was the mother of John the Baptist (Luke 1:39-56). By Protestant accounts, Mary was not a perpetual virgin and later became the mother of other sons and daughters (Matthew 13:55-56). Mary was a widow at the time of Jesus' death, and while on the cross, Jesus committed her care to the Apostle John (John 19:25-27).

On the other hand, Luke had a different perspective and focused on the destiny of his audience. We know from the study that Luke was a physician and that he carefully investigated things from his scientific mindset (including the life of Christ) and wrote the books of Luke and Acts (Colossians 4:14, Luke 1:1-4, Acts 1:1). It is also clear that Luke's readers were less concerned about the fulfillment of Jewish prophecy (as were Matthew's), and his genealogy focuses on Jesus' descent from God.

It did not emphasize Jesus being the descendant of King David.

I especially find it significant interest that Matthew and Luke both showed that Joseph was a legal parent, not a just genetic parent to Jesus. While Jesus was miraculously conceived of Mary through the Holy Spirit, they both used the human format to display the destiny of Jesus.

By being Mary's husband, Joseph was considered the father of Jesus. Since Jesus was born into Joseph's family, he was a legal heir. Through Joseph, Jesus obtained a rightful claim to the throne of David.

It appears at first glance that both Matthew and Luke get tripped up on the question of "who is Joseph's father?" Here we depend on more scholarly resources; the Jerusalem Talmud indicates that Mary was the daughter of Heli (Hagigah, Book 77, 4). Joseph was the son-in-law of Heli. Luke could rightfully call Joseph the "son of Heli" because this complied with the use of the word "son" at that time. Moreover, designating a son-in-law as a son had scriptural precedent. Thus, we conclude that Joseph was the son of Jacob and the son-in-law of Heli.

Also, interesting to note is an unusual curse that explains the necessity of the focused destiny of Jesus Christ. You don't often hear this topic addressed, but Jeremiah 36:1-32 shows us why there had to be a virgin birth to bring the Messiah to earth. Here's the problem, Jehoiakim was the king of Israel, and he angered God by burning a scroll that Jeremiah the Prophet wrote. God cursed Jehoiakim by indicating that none of his children would sit on the throne of David (Jeremiah 36:29-31). Although Jehoiakim had children, scripture shows that none of them ever reigned as King David had.

However, Joseph, the father of Jesus, was one of Jehoiakim's descendants (through Jeconiah). Joseph's offspring could not claim David's throne because of the curse. Jesus laid claim to the throne of David (Luke 1:32, Acts 2:30, Hebrews 12:2). If Jesus had been born of Joseph, the curse would have been a contradiction. Also, God had promised David that one of his physical descendants would reign on the throne of his kingdom forever (2 Samuel 7:12-13). Joseph was excluded from being the genetic father of the future king of Israel. That meant it was impossible to fulfill the requirements of both curse and promise by natural means. One man had to be both heir to and offspring of David without being the genetic descendant of Jehoiakim. This problem required a divine solution.

Joseph was one of Jehoiakim's offspring (through Solomon), but Mary was not. She was a descendant of Nathan, one of David's other sons (Luke 3:31). God's promise to David was fulfilled because Mary was the biological parent of Jesus. Thus, the virgin birth addressed the curse God had pronounced upon Jehoiakim while providing a solution at the same time.

It behooves me to note Paul's instructions to a young pastor named Timothy and how quickly one can get sidetracked from the important when focusing on the irrelevant. 1 Timothy 1: 3-6 As I urged you upon my departure for Macedonia, remain on at Ephesus so that you may instruct certain men not to teach strange doctrines, nor to pay attention to myths and endless genealogies, which give rise to mere speculation rather than furthering the administration of God which is by faith. But the goal of our instruction is love from a pure heart and a good conscience, and a sincere faith. For some men, straying from these things has turned aside into fruitless discussion.

Bibliography

(The Message (MSG) Copyright © 1993, 1994, 1995, 1996, 2000, 2001, 2002 by Eugene H. Peterson)

That word above all earthly powers, no thanks to them, abideth; the Spirit and the gifts are ours, thru him who with us sideth. Let goods and kindred go, this mortal life also; The body they may kill; God's truth abideth still; his kingdom is forever.

The Three Tenses of Salvation, adapted from Major Bible Themes, edited by John F. Walvoord, Zondervan, Grand Rapids, 1973, p. 184.

MARTIN LUTHER - A MIGHTY FORTRESS IS OUR GOD   LYRICS. https://www.songlyrics.com/martin-luther/a-mighty-fortress-is-our-god-lyrics/

Think about that for a moment in light of whom you are and the people you interact with regularly

You Can Increase Your Intelligence: 5 Ways to Maximize....

https://blogs.scientificamerican.com/guest-blog/you-can-increase-your-intelligence-5-ways-to-maximize-your-cognitive-potential/

There are three stages of salvation that create a wonderful package that God has gifted to us in Christ when we receive His finished works. The first is in the past tense, where God in Christ has saved us from the penalty of sin,

Soteriology - The Doctrine of Salvation | Bible.org. https://bible.org/article/soteriology-doctrine-salvation

Let's look at Matthew's five women in his record and why he does so. Firstly, there is Tamar in Genesis 38:6-30. Tamar was the daughter-in-law of Judah. She was also a childless widow who was given to her brother-in-law after her husband's death. By this marriage, her offspring would continue the name and inheritance of the deceased.

A STUDY OF THE HARMONY OF THE GOSPELS. http://www.vscoc.org/Workbooks/Harmony_bk 1.htm

being Mary's husband, Joseph was considered the father of Jesus. Since Jesus was born into Joseph's family, he was a legal heir. Through Joseph, Jesus obtained a rightful claim to the throne of David.

Joseph, son of Jacob: Family tree by Cecelia HOGUE.... https://gw.geneanet.org/chogue?lang=en&n=jacob&oc=1&p=joseph+son+of

instruct certain men not to teach strange doctrines, nor to pay attention to myths and endless genealogies, which give rise to mere speculation rather than furthering the administration of God

Luke 1 - The Birth of John the Baptist. http://ocbubble.com/nautilus/videos/Luke/Luke%201.doc

For some men, straying from these things, have turned aside to fruitless discussion.

1 Timothy 1:3-7 - NAS - As I urged you Lit https://www.christianity.com/bible/nas/1-timothy/1-3-7

Old fakir (a Muslim Sufi ascetic in the Middle East and South Asia).

What is a simple definition of ethics?

https://morethingsjapanese.com/what-is-a-simple-definition-of-ethics/

And we know that in all things, God works for the good of those who love him, who have been called according to his purpose.

Romans 8:29 Meaning of Conformed to the Image ... – Connect US.

https://connectusfund.org/romans-8-29-meaning-of-conformed-to-the-image-of-his-son

Chapter Nine

Monkey's Paw

What is a monkey paw, you might ask? The monkey's paw is a symbol of desire and greed. It is said that whoever wields it or is the owner can wish for anything that his or her heart desires and have absolute unrestricted control to make it happen. This power makes the paw alluring, even to unselfish people who desire nothing and have everything they need. You might be taken off guard, questioning why I am mentioning a monkey paw and its relevance. Please bear with me as it will all make sense.

One of my all-time favorite short stories is a British story entitled "The Monkey's Paw."

In the story, there are three wishes granted to the owner of the monkey's paw. Each wish comes with an enormous price as it alters one's destiny. Please allow me to summarize the story for you.

The story's main characters are Mr. and Mrs. White and their adult son, Herbert. While a close friend of the Whites, Sergeant-Major Morris is a British officer in the regiments of India. He introduces them to the monkey's paw and tells them of its mysterious powers to grant three wishes to the

213

holder. During his journeys, the Major obtained the monkey's paw from an old fakir (a Muslim Sufi ascetic in the Middle East and South Asia).

Having had a bad experience using the paw Sergeant-Major Morris directly throws it into the fire in disgust as he explains its powers. While Mr. White quickly retrieves it, Morris warns of the imminence of pain and suffering while in his possession.

Mr. White's first wish is for the sum of £200, desiring to clear the mortgage on their home. The following day soon after, his son Herbert leaves for work, and there is a message about his tragic death. The young man is killed in a machinery accident at the factory where he works. The Whites receive compensation for their son's death of £200 from his employer.

Ten days after the son's funeral, Mrs. White, overcome with grief, begs her husband to use the paw to bring back their son. While Mr. White is reluctant to do so, he makes their second wish. Momentarily after the wish is made, there is a knock at the door and Mrs.

White finds herself struggling to open it. Supposing it to be their son, Mr. White refrains himself. He cannot allow his son to be revived in the appearance he last saw him. Mr. White was required to identify his son's body and recalls how mutilated it was by accident. Not to mention it has been over a week since his burial, and it would be far too hideous for his wife to see. As Mrs. White struggles to open the door, Mr. White makes his third wish, and the knocking ceases. Mrs. White finally opens the door, and the couple is pleasantly surprised to find no one there.

The story's underlying theme is in the spell the old fakir casts upon the paw. It is meant to show how destiny rules people's lives, and if interfered with it, there might be a great sorrow to pay.

Having said all of that (with such a shrilling example), allow me to make this proclamation as with the boom of a cannon "The devil is a liar and the father of it." The Apostle Paul speaking to the Galatians, says it this way in Galatians 1:6-8; 3:1-3 I am astonished that you are so quickly deserting the one who called you to live in the grace of Christ and is turning to a different gospel- which is no gospel at all. Some people are throwing you into confusion and are trying to pervert the Gospel of Christ.

But even if an angel from heaven or we should preach a

gospel other than the one we preached to you, let them be under God's curse! You foolish Galatians! Who has bewitched you? Before your very eyes, Jesus Christ was clearly portrayed as crucified. I want to learn just one thing from you: Did you receive the Spirit by the works of the law or by believing what you heard? Are you so foolish? After beginning by means of the Spirit, are you now trying to finish by means of the flesh? What had the Galatians done that was so horrible it required a "tongue lashing" from Paul? They had received the Gospel with its finished works in Christ and then began to look back at their religious ways, thinking maybe it wasn't enough. Perhaps we should add some good works or rituals to the mix. Paul says it so bluntly, who has bewitched you? In other words, what kind of a trance were you in?

I believe we are all great "mixers," but that only makes things more difficult for us. We have to keep our eyes focused on our destiny, not our past.

Romans 8:28-30 unpacks a beautiful secret that most Christians miss because of the sandwiched theology. It reads like this: And we know that in all things God works for the good of those who love him, who have been called according to his purpose.

Verse 29-For those God foreknew, He also predestined to be conformed to the image of his Son, that he might be the firstborn among many brothers and sisters. And those he predestined, he also called; those he called, he also justified; those he justified, he also glorified.

If you don't get anything out of this book, I want you to absorb the center line in verse 29. To be conformed to the image of his son. Can you say it out loud so the person next to you hears it? I believe that verse is meant to change your life forever. That verse is so powerful that if we strive to do it, we will never stray from God's will for our lives- ever again.

The practical question then becomes, "how"- how do we go about conforming to the image of his son? If you haven't picked up on it yet, I love to pick apart the "how" questions. We know that there is always a central truth when studying the Bible, but the applications vary. So, the way you apply this truth is different from how I would use it.

In 2 Corinthians 3: 17 and 18, Paul likens the process to Moses' encounter with God at the burning bush. If you recall the story in Exodus 34 of Moses' encounter with the glory of God, his face shone so brightly that he wore a veil when addressing the people of Israel. See if you can connect the dots in Paul's application of conforming to the image of his son. It reads this way: Now the Lord is the Spirit, and where the Spirit of the Lord is, there is liberty. But we all, with unveiled faces, beholding as in a mirror the glory of the Lord, are being transformed into the same image from glory to glory, just as from the Lord, the Spirit.

Did you catch the present tense as he begins- Now? The Lord is the Spirit, and where the Spirit of the Lord is, there is liberty. Why is that important? Because the process will always occur in God's presence, and since his Spirit dwells within all believers, we don't have to go up to the mountain or down to the valley. Please don't miss the last part of that verse- where the Spirit of the Lord is; there is liberty. Liberty means a lot of different things to a lot of other folks, but to God, it always means the same thing. Freedom is becoming who God has made you in Christ. You will never become a whole person outside of Christ.

Then Paul concludes, but we all, with unveiled face, beholding as in a mirror the glory of the Lord, are being transformed into the same image from glory to glory, just as from the Lord, the Spirit.

218

He says with unveiled faces, depicting our complete transparency before God, beholding as in a mirror. You have to keep in mind that mirrors in those days had a dim and somewhat blurry image but an unmistakable reflection. We discussed in previous chapters that the word glory means "manifested excellence of God." Last but not least, we are being transformed into the same image during the process of glory to glory in God's presence.

Have you discovered that there is a difference between transformation and change? Do you know of times when you went through a change process- change of habit, change of mind, change of place, or change from your hand to mine?

You experienced change alright, but it wasn't lasting because you weren't transformed. Transforming change can only take place in God's presence, in God's time, and on God's terms, and it just doesn't happens any other way.

Did you realize that the process of sanctification- that present tense part of being saved means that you and I are "set apart" for God's usefulness? Think about that for just a moment. What kinds of things do you set apart for your usefulness? You set apart a hairbrush, a toothbrush, spectacles, contact lens, something you take into your person, and the list goes on and on. But Almighty God has set you and me apart for Himself. How awesome is that?

Until you realize that you have been set apart for God's usefulness, you probably will never enter into personal holiness. You might attempt in your strength, but you'll soon find yourself becoming self-righteous instead. This venue helps us a springboard into our final chapter because none of this becomes possible without a genuine relationship.

Bibliography

old fakir (a Muslim Sufi ascetic in the Middle East and South Asia).

What is a simple definition of ethics...

https://morethingsjapanese.com/what-is-a-simple-definition-of-ethics/

And we know that in all things God works for the good of those who love him, who have been called according to his purpose.

Romans 8:29 Meaning of Conformed to the Image ... - ConnectUS. https://connectusfund.org/romans-8-29-meaning-of-conformed-to-the-image-of-his-son

The wrath of God is being revealed from heaven against all the godlessness and wickedness of people, who suppress the truth by their wickedness since what may be known about God is plain to them because God has made it

Daily Devotion: Suppressing the Truth (Romans 1:18-23).

https://www.raystedman.org/daily-devotions/romans-1to8/suppressing-the-truth

seen, being understood from what has been made so that people are without excuse. For although they knew God, they neither glorified him as God nor gave thanks to him, but their thinking became futile, and their foolish hearts were darkened. Although they claimed to be wise, they became fools

The wrath of God is being revealed from heaven against...

https://ourcog.org/the-wrath-of-god-is-being-revealed-from-heaven-against/

They exchanged the truth about God for a lie and worshiped and served created things rather than the Creator—who is forever praised. Amen.

Daily Devotion: God Gave Them Over (Romans 1:24-32).

https://www.raystedman.org/daily-devotions/romans-1to8/god-gave-them-over

I've always had some difficulty with these verses in light of the loving character of God, but when combined with the nature of a God of holiness and justice

So that men are without excuse. | tallandrew.

https://onliving.wordpress.com/2010/05/22/so-that-men-are-without-excuse/

If we claim to be without sin, we deceive ourselves, and the truth is not in us. If we confess our sins, he is faithful and just and will forgive us our sins and purify us from all unrighteousness. If we claim we have not sinned, we make him out to be a liar, and his word is not in us.

Marching in the Light: 1 John 1.1-10 - Pepperdine University.

https://digitalcommons.pepperdine.edu/cgi/viewcontent.cgi?referer=&httpsredir=1&article=1031&context=leaven

If you do this, then do that, but don't do this, then presto. You are right in the eyes of God.

CHRISTIANITY IS NOT A RELIGION-IS A PRACTICE OF FAITH...

https://thomasgoodmanblog.wordpress.com/2017/08/08/christianity-is-not-a-religion-is-a-practice-of-f-aith/

Look at what Jesus said in Matthew 22:37-40:

They Might Be Giants - The Caffeinated Theologian.

https://caffeinatedtheologian.wordpress.com/2015/01/13/th
ey-might-be-giants/

The Apostle Peter was martyred in 64 AD at the hands of Nero, and according to Eusebius, Peter thought himself unworthy to be crucified in the same manner as his Master and asked to be crucified "head downward."

WHAT HAPPENED TO THE TWELVE APOSTLES? HOW DO THEIR DEATHS...

https://gospelsoundersministry.org/wp-
content/uploads/2019/12/What-Happened-to-the-Twelve-
Apostles.pdf

Even now, there is no condemnation for those who are in Christ Jesus (Rom. 8:1). He has made us acceptable in the Beloved (Eph. 1:6). Indeed, we are complete in Him (Col. 2:10).

The Infinite Has Accepted YOU! – Finding Our Way Home.

https://stephennewdellsfindingthewayhome2017.wordpress.
com/the-infinite-has-accepted-you/

The story was written by author William Wymark Jacobs and was first published in England in 1902 (Jacobs, W. W.;

Parker, Louis N. (1910). The Monkey's Paw: A Story in Three Scenes. London: Samuel French, Ltd. P. 5.)

Chapter Ten

David by Michelangelo

All in the Relationship

Our final chapter of the book addresses the utmost essential ingredient in life, unmatched by any religion or personal opinion. It is the one thing that makes successful people who they are and carries them into legendary status. It's not just relationships in a networking sense, but genuine relationships. It's the one thing that has reminded me of God's love and involvement in humanity throughout the development stages of my life. Looking back, there has been a pathway for people who have made a difference in forming who God wanted me to become. The people in my family, either directly or indirectly, showed me how to pray or become sensitive to the presence of God in my life. Encounters with extraordinary people helped me see the true character of God.

It's funny, isn't it, that we, in a way, are born alone and die alone while the people around us become a figment of our dream or imagination, and yet these feelings and thoughts are not true. Even the staunchest critic or someone who doesn't feel the presence of God in their life cannot die the almost magical or metaphysical nature of family. Family is something we all want and crave for. Even though not

227

everything about them would be perfect, there are still strong bonds of affection. The family system, sadly, day by day, is scattered in the wind without the hope of ever truly coming back.

It is ironic though the family system is broken apart while coinciding with the fact that churches are empty. One of the most essential things about the bible is that it always wants to keep the family unit intact, for that is the best way to live your life. For as long as the family is together, the chances of committing real sins become lesser. Here are just some things the bible talks about when it comes to family.

The very first people on earth formed a family. From the beginning, God blessed and encouraged families, commanding Adam and Eve to "be fruitful, and multiply, and replenish the earth" (Genesis 1:28)

The family will always play a big part in our lives; hence it is saddening to see in the modern age that the family system is falling apart. The core of what makes us whole and united as one is vanishing in front of our eyes, and many of us are giving in. Yet there is hope that with Christ's guidance, we can overcome the impossible. We, as the children of heaven, have always defined ourselves with the ability to overcome the impossible, but we have lost our way. But our proudest achievements cannot be behind us as our destiny hangs in the balance. Made in the lord's image, we must show our true spirit and bring our brothers and sisters who have lost their way back on the right path. I hope this book can contribute to a small part of it.

People like Mother Teresa, which I don't often talk about, but in appearance, a frail and bent woman with wrinkled hands and kind eyes who changed my view of what it meant to love God while serving people. I think all of us would agree that life is either enriched or forever stained by our involvement with other people. Getting to know people is an awkward or an awesome process, but that experience impacts us throughout our lifetime. While the Focal Point of our destiny is all about relationships, it is not just about human relationships. We need to understand that there is a widening scope of who we are as we envelop in a dimension beyond the physical. I know that sounds way out there, but hang with me a bit and allow me to explain.

If I were describing a person in a holistic sense, I could say that I am a spirit that lives in a body expressing myself with a soul. While that gives light to the eternal likeness of our Creator, it says nothing of a relationship with him.

Parson To Person: Three Things God Wants You To Know About Life

Throughout the ages, God has reviewed himself to humanity with a promise of redemption. From the time of Adam and Eve, God promised that sin would no longer wedge our relationship but that he would, at the right time, create an eternal bridge. In the process, humanity has sought to fill that void by suppressing the truth of God's presence that is all around us.

Let's read Romans 1:18-25 to clarify. The wrath of God is being revealed from heaven against all the godlessness and wickedness of people, who suppress the truth by their wickedness since what may be known about God is plain to them because God has made it simple to them. Since the world's creation, God's invisible qualities—his eternal power and divine nature—have been seen, being understood from what has been made so that people are without excuse. For although they knew God, they neither glorified him as God nor gave thanks to him, but their thinking became futile, and their foolish hearts were darkened.

Although they claimed to be wise, they became fools and exchanged the glory of the immortal God for images made to look like mortal human beings and birds and animals and reptiles. Therefore, God gave them over in the sinful desires of their hearts to sexual impurity for the degrading of their bodies with one another. They exchanged the truth about God for a lie and worshiped and served created things rather than the Creator—who is forever praised. Amen.

I've always had some difficulty with these verses in light of the loving character of God, but when combined with the nature of a God of holiness and justice, it makes perfect sense. The finality of this passage disturbs a lot of people. Paul doesn't hold back in describing how wicked the human heart is, and he concludes by saying people are without excuse.

The question that has always been posted at this point is, 'what about the lost tribe in the Amazon that has never heard of Jesus? '

To say that God gives knowledge and grace to all as he reveals himself to us just doesn't seem to be enough to explain the how and why question that nag us. I believe as we respond to the truth in its most basic form, God continues to reveal himself to us in extended ways that bring us to the message of the Gospel.

The Gospel begins with the message of hope that God promised to Adam and Eve in the garden. Genesis 3:15 And I will put enmity between you and the woman, and between your offspring and hers; he will crush your head, and you will strike his heel." Here the mystery of the incarnate Son of God is foreshadowed, and the seed of the woman creates an eternal bridge. Galatians 4:4 says, when the set time had fully come, God sent his Son, born of a woman, born under the Law.

Our hope began with the voice of a loving father calling his children after they had sinned- Genesis 3:9 Where are you? (Literally, "what are you doing over there?") That's what makes Christianity different from other religions- a loving God reaches out to bridge the gap between Himself and fallen humanity.

Religion can be defined as a belief system with a moral code of conduct, whereby a person must adhere to gain acceptance. While God began to separate a group of people unto him by giving the Law to Moses, it was only to show them how utterly impossible it was to keep it. If you can't find the right standing with a holy God by doing good works, then you need a Savior. A Savior bridges the gap between you and God and becomes a perfect replacement for all your brokenness.

The Gospel begins with the Law, but it doesn't stay there.

The Law was meant to show us our need for a Savior. 1 John 1:8-10 says it this way: If we claim to be without sin, we deceive ourselves and the truth is not in us. If we confess our sins, he is faithful and just and will forgive us our sins and purify us from all unrighteousness. If we claim we have not sinned, we make him out to be a liar, and his word is not in us.

During the earthly ministry of Jesus Christ, a group of corrupt religious leaders called the Pharisees sought to keep the Law given to Moses and the prophets (known as Torah). They and other pious Jewish rabbis wanted to make sure those laws were observed correctly, so they wrote a commentary on 613 laws interpreting them (known as the Talmud). There was already an earlier commentary called the Oral Law or Mishnah, which was supposed to be an unwritten interpretation of the Torah; it had several hundred regulations.

At any rate, Jesus hated the way the Pharisees used the people's love for God to control them. This kind of love isn't genuine; it's more like fearful respect. 1 John 4:18 says this about "perfect love":

There is no fear in love, but perfect love casts out fear

because fear involves punishment, and the one who fears is not perfected in love. Jesus knew how these controlling religious laws emptied the people of an authentic relationship with God and reduced their devotion to a mere formula.

When you practice outside of the relationship, religion will constantly be degraded to a mathematical formula. If you do this, then do that, but don't do this, then presto. You are right in the eyes of God. You have missed the point with all the confusion about your good intentions. God wants so much more than a mathematical formula; he wants a real relationship.

Read Romans 5:7-8 For one will hardly die for a righteous man; though perhaps for the good man someone would dare even to die. But God demonstrates His love toward us in that while we were yet sinners, Christ died for us.

How awesome is that? While we were at our ugliest point, Almighty God demonstrated his love for us in the substitutionary atonement of Jesus Christ.

In the Law, God said, "Remember the Sabbath day and keep it holy." The Sabbath was supposed to be a way to break from work and refocus on essential things like spending time with family and God. However, the true meaning was misinterpreted in the formula. You can't build a relationship without quality time. I also sincerely believe that you cannot share the entire message of the Gospel without beginning with the Law. The 10 Commandments are all about relationships, and they are about improving our relationship with God or other people.

Look at what Jesus said in Matthew 22:37-40: You must love the Lord your God with all your heart, all your soul, and all your mind. This is the first and greatest commandment. A second is equally important: Love your neighbor as yourself. The entire Law and all the demands of the prophets are based on these two commandments. Wow, can you absorb the magnitude of these verses? The Apostle Paul should have been called "the finisher" because he always took the application to the most practical extent.

In Romans 13:9-10, he connects the dots for us in this way: For the commandments say, "You must not commit adultery. You must not murder. You must not steal. You must not covet."

These—and other such commandments—are summed up in this one commandment: "Love your neighbor as yourself."

Love does no wrong to others, so love fulfills the requirements of God's Law.

So, the sum of the Law, if we return to our mathematical formula, equals love, love for God, and love for others.

The Law is about relationships, vertical and horizontal. It is about our vertical relationship with our Creator and our horizontal relationships with other people- strangest enough gives us the image of a cross. The cross is where God spoke directly to the problem and put a period at the end of it. 1 Peter 3:18 says: For Christ also suffered once for sins, the righteous for the unrighteous, to bring you to God. He was put to death in the body but made alive in the Spirit.

Let's revisit the verse from Romans 5:7-8: For one will hardly die for a righteous man; though perhaps for the good man someone would dare even to die. But God demonstrates His own love toward us in that while we were yet sinners, Christ died for us. Imagine yourself as an upper-class intellectual during the first century living in Rome during (or shortly after) the death of Jesus Christ. What might be your response if someone told you that Christianity would become the national religion by the third century and that the emperor himself would be a follower of this man Jesus

Christ? You would probably be significantly shocked by unbelief.

While considering relationships in light of God and humanity, have you ever thought about what happened to the 12 Apostles of Jesus Christ following the resurrection? History tells us quite a lot about them and the emperors that ruled over Rome after that. For the sake of boring you, we know that Emperor Nero was the first and most brutal of all persecuting Roman Emperors, and we know that both Peter and Paul were put to death by his orders. Even though historical records show us several events surrounding the Apostles' lives, the details are not altogether constant.

Let us consider the introduction to Romans 5:7-8. For one will hardly die for a righteous man, though perhaps for the good man, someone would dare even to die. I find it extraordinary that each of the 12 Apostles had a willful choice to deny their faith in Jesus Christ and live, but instead chose to suffer horribly as martyrs. We see in Acts 7:58-60 that the first martyr was Stephen and that a young man named Saul was present as the witnesses laid their garments at his feet.

The second to be martyred was James in Acts 12:2 (about

237

44-45 AD) at the hands of Herod Agrippa; it reads: He killed James, the brother of John, with the sword. Also noted was that both Clement of Alexandria and Eusebius (Ecclesiastical History II.2) reported that after seeing the courage and recanting Spirit of James, the executioner was so convinced of Christ's resurrection that he was executed with him. Simply remarkable!

The Apostle Peter was martyred in 64 AD at the hands of Nero, and according to Eusebius, Peter thought himself unworthy to be crucified in the same manner as his Master and asked to be crucified "head downward." As noted, Paul also suffered a martyr's death at the hands of Nero in 67AD.

In 70 AD, Andrew, who introduced his brother Peter to Christ, was martyred six years after Peter. After preaching Christ's resurrection to the Scythians and Thracians, he too was crucified for his faith. As Hippolytus tells us, Andrew was hanged on an olive tree at Patrae, a town in Achaia.

Also, in 70AD, Thomas was known as "doubting Thomas" because of his reluctance to believe the other apostles' witness of the resurrection. In John 20:25, he says: "Unless I see in his hands the mark of the nails, and place my finger into the mark of the nails, and place my hand into his side, I will never believe." After this, Christ appeared to Thomas, and he believed unto death. Thomas sealed his testimony as he was thrust through with pine spears, tormented with red-hot plates, and burned alive.

In 54AD, Philip was martyred. Do you recall in John 14:8–9 when Christ corrected Philip when he asked: Philip said to him, "Lord, show us the Father, and it is enough for us." Jesus said to him, "Have I been with you so long, and you still do not know me, Philip? Whoever has seen me has seen the Father. How can you say, 'Show us the Father? Philip saw the glory of Christ after the resurrection and was undoubtedly amazed at Christ's response to his request. Philip evangelized in Phrygia, where hostile Jews had him tortured and then crucified.

Between 60-70 AD, Matthew, the tax collector, desperately wanted the Jews to accept Christ. He wrote The Gospel According to Matthew about ten years before his death. Within its pages, one can see the faith for which he spilled his blood. In Matthew 28:20, the resurrected Christ says: "And behold, I am with you always, to the end of the age." These comforting words likely sustained Matthew when we were beheaded at Nad-Davar.

In 70 AD, Nathanael, whose name means "gift of God," was indeed given as a gift to the Church through his martyrdom. In John 1:49, Nathanael was the first to profess Christ: Nathanael answered him, "Rabbi, you are the Son of God! You are the King of Israel!" He later paid for this profession through a hideous death. Unwilling to recant his proclamation of a risen Christ, he was flayed and then crucified.

In 63 AD, James was the appointed head of the Jerusalem church for many years after Christ's death. He undoubtedly contacted many hostile Jews who, in Matthew 27:25, said: And all the people answered, "His blood be on our children and on us!" To force James to deny Christ's resurrection, these men positioned him at the top of the Temple in Jerusalem. Unwilling to deny what he knew to be accurate; James was cast down from the Temple and finally beaten to death with a fuller's club to the head.

In 74 AD, Simon was a Jewish zealot who strived to free his people from Roman oppression. After seeing with his own eyes that Christ had been resurrected, he became a zealot of the Gospel.

Historians tell of the many places Simon proclaimed the

good news of Christ's resurrection: Egypt, Cyrene, Africa, Mauritania, Britain, Lybia, and Persia. His martyrdom, brought about by a governor in Syria, verified his testimony for Christ.

In 72AD, in John 14:22, Judas asked Jesus: Judas (not Iscariot) said to him, "Lord, how is it that you will manifest yourself to us, and not to the world?" After he witnessed Christ's resurrection, Judas knew the answer. He preached the risen Christ amid pagan priests in Mesopotamia. He was eventually beaten to death with sticks, showing to the world that Christ was indeed Lord and God.

Acts 1:26 recorded how Matthias replaced Judas Iscariot (the betrayer of Christ who hanged himself) as the twelfth apostle of Christ. In 70AD, he is said by Eusebius to have preached in Ethiopia, and he was later stoned while hanging upon a cross.

John is the only one of the twelve apostles who died a natural death. Although he did not die a martyr's death, he did live a martyr's life. He was exiled to the Island of Patmos during the reign of Emperor Domitian for his proclamation of the risen Christ. There, he wrote the last book of the Bible, Revelation. Some traditions say he was thrown into boiling oil before the Latin Gate. While this didn't kill him, it likely scarred him for life (95AD).

We are encouraged not to die for their lies, half-truths, or fabrications. While the Apostles could be seen in the same light as other religious extremists, the difference is that they were not receiving their faith second-handed, but they were validating those beliefs by their deaths.

So then, as Genesis 1:26 told us, God tells us to make human beings in our image and likeness, and while we don't know all the aspects that cover, we know that we are eternal spirits and that our earthly bodies are the only temporary. We know that, like God, we are relational beings and can discern right from wrong. We also know that we can give and receive love. We understand that the image of God has been damaged and distorted in our humanity by sin and that God sent His Son Jesus Christ to restore that image by his death, burial, and resurrection.

While we are made in the image of God, we will never be higher than the Creator. This desire to be a god arises every time we are tempted to take control of our destiny and the people around us. Your destiny in life will never be about comfort and self-satisfaction but about conforming to the image of Christ. God desires that all of us grow up and become like Jesus in this world. You are a uniquely gifted person, and your genuine personality should reflect your Creator's inner glow and reflection.

As Colossians, 1:26- 27 proclaims the mystery which has been hidden from the past ages and generations but has now been manifested to His saints, to whom God willed to make known what is the riches of the glory of this mystery among the Gentiles which is Christ in you, the hope of glory. I hope you will stop to ponder that verse time and again because Christ indwells every believer and allows us to become the hope of the manifested excellence of all that God has placed in Jesus Christ. We are like a mirror reflecting his image to this world. Even in all our blemishes and shortcomings, it is his righteousness that pleases God and makes us complete. Even now, there is no condemnation for those who are in Christ Jesus (Rom. 8:1). He has made us acceptable in the Beloved (Eph. 1:6). Indeed, we are complete in Him (Col. 2:10).

1 John 4:16-17 illustrates our destiny best when he tells us that God is love, and if we are born of Him, we should be like Him in this world. We have come to know and have believed in the love which God has for us. God is love, and

the one who abides in love abides in God, and God abides in him. By this, love is perfected with us so that we may have confidence in the Day of Judgment; because as He is, so also are we in this world. That brings us to our final point that God wants you to know about life.

While Christ is the focal point of your destiny in all relationships, the key to our successfulness in this life is in "conforming to His image.

By this is love perfected with us, so that we may have confidence for the Day of Judgment, because as he is, so also are we in this world. (1 John 4:17, English Standard Version) AMEN.

Bibliography

The wrath of God is being revealed from heaven against all the godlessness and wickedness of people, who suppress the truth by their wickedness since what may be known about God is plain to them because God has made it

Daily Devotion: Suppressing the Truth (Romans 1:18-23). https://www.raystedman.org/daily-devotions/romans-1to8/suppressing-the-truth

seen, being understood from what has been made so that people are without excuse. For although they knew God, they neither glorified him as God nor gave thanks to him, but their thinking became futile, and their foolish hearts were darkened. Although they claimed to be wise, they became fools

The wrath of God is being revealed from heaven against .... https://ourcog.org/the-wrath-of-god-is-being-revealed-from-heaven-against/

They exchanged the truth about God for a lie and worshiped and served created things rather than the Creator—who is forever praised. Amen.

Daily Devotion: God Gave Them Over (Romans 1:24-32). https://www.raystedman.org/daily-devotions/romans-1to8/god-gave-them-over

I've always had some difficulty with these verses in light of the loving character of God, but when combined with the nature of a God of holiness and justice

So that men are without excuse. | tallandrew. https://onliving.wordpress.com/2010/05/22/so-that-men-are-without-excuse/

If we claim to be without sin, we deceive ourselves and the truth is not in us. If we confess our sins, he is faithful and just and will forgive us our sins and purify us from all unrighteousness. If we claim we have not sinned, we make him out to be a liar, and his word is not in us.

Marching in the Light: 1 John 1.1-10 - Pepperdine University. https://digitalcommons.pepperdine.edu/cgi/viewcontent.cgi?referer=&httpsredir=1&article=1031&context=leaven

If you do this, then do that, but don't do this, then presto. You are right in the eyes of God.

CHRISTIANITY IS NOT A RELIGION-IS A PRACTICE

OF   FAITH
.... https://thomasgoodmanblog.wordpress.com/2017/08/08/
christianity-is-not-a-religion-is-a-practice-of-f-aith/

Look at what Jesus said in Matthew 22:37-40:

They   Might   Be   Giants   -   The   Caffeinated
Theologian. https://caffeinatedtheologian.wordpress.com/2
015/01/13/they-might-be-giants/

*The Apostle Peter was martyred in 64 AD at the hands of
Nero, and according to Eusebius, Peter thought himself
unworthy to be crucified in the same manner as his Master
and asked to be crucified "head downward."*

WHAT HAPPENED TO THE TWELVE APOSTLES?
HOW   DO   THEIR   DEATHS
.... https://gospelsoundersministry.org/wp-
content/uploads/2019/12/What-Happened-to-the-Twelve-
Apostles.pdf

*Even now, there is no condemnation for those who are in
Christ Jesus (Rom. 8:1). He has made us acceptable in the
Beloved (Eph. 1:6). Indeed, we are complete in Him (Col.
2:10).*

The Infinite Has Accepted YOU! – Finding Our Way

Home. https://stephennewdellsfindingthewayhome2017.wordpress.com/the-infinite-has-accepted-you/

https://www.churchofjesuschrist.org/comeuntochrist/uk/beliefs/holy-bible/bible-topics/what-does-the-bible-teach-about-family

www.ingramcontent.com/pod-product-compliance
Lightning Source LLC
Chambersburg PA
CBHW070919120626
46546CB00001B/327